OBAMA'S FOUR HORSEMEN

OBAMA'S FOUR HORSEMEN

THE DISASTERS UNLEASHED BY OBAMA'S REELECTION

DAVID HARSANYI

Since 1947
REGNERY
PUBLISHING, INC.
An Eagle Publishing Company • Washington, DC

Cataloging-in-Publication data on file with the Library of Congress

ISBN 978-1-62157-067-7

Published in the United States by

Regnery Publishing, Inc.
One Massachusetts Avenue NW
Washington, DC 20001
www.Regnery.com

Manufactured in the United States of America

10 9 8 7 6 5 4 3 2 1

Books are available in quantity for promotional or premium use. Write to Director of Special Sales, Regnery Publishing, Inc., One Massachusetts Avenue NW, Washington, DC 20001, for information on discounts and terms or call (202) 216-0600.

Distributed to the trade by

Perseus Distribution
250 West 57th Street
New York, NY 10107

For Mom and Dad

CONTENTS

CHAPTER ONE

HIGHWAY TO HELL

"In my own time, governments have taken the place of people.
They have also taken the place of God. Governments speak for people,
dream for them, and determine, absurdly, their lives and deaths.

This new worship of government is one of the subjects in this book.
It is this worship I lack. I have no reverence for the all-powerful and
bewildered face of Government. I see it as a lessening of the human
being, and a final looting of his birthright—the survival of his young.
I see it as an ogre with despair in its eyes."
—BEN HECHT IN HIS PREFACE TO *PERFIDY*, 1961

The Church of the Greater Good

The Four Horsemen of the Apocalypse? The Book of Revelation?
Fire? Brimstone? Armageddon? The Last Judgment?

Really, David?

Yes, really.

As metaphors go, it's an entirely apt one. To begin with, Con-
quest, Famine, War, Death—the four horsemen of the Obama Era—
are coming, and they are coming in the form of a national debt
disaster, an epidemic of government dependence, an erosion of our

world standing, and a nihilistic view about the value of human life. If our federal government had been inclined to do anything to avoid these impending catastrophes—and I'm not sure it ever was—that day has now passed. Barack Obama's reelection ensures we'll be dealing with some level of societal instability and economic calamity in the future. No, these calamities won't transform us into Bangladesh, and they won't mean the United States will cease to exist. They will only mean that this particular iteration of the United States will be no more.

Change, of course, doesn't always imply impending disaster. Americans seldom accept that terrible events can befall them. We have solid reasons not to. Truth is, I have always been somewhat of a utopian regarding our prospects. I operated under the rosy assumption that our free markets, individual liberty, technological superiority, astonishing wealth, and Constitutional protections (however eroded they may have become) would allow us to adapt to or overcome nearly anything—recessions; wars; terror attacks; demographic shifts; environmental disaster; and, the most treacherous of all threats, Washington. Regrettably, I underestimated Washington.

President Barack Obama didn't invent the impending disasters America faces—not our debt problem, not our welfare state—but he did accelerate nearly every one of them. It's not only that the president's progressive politics have battered economic dynamism, hamstrung capitalism, and discredited the importance of meritocracy; it's that, in the Obama era, the relationship between the average American citizen and his government has been transformed forever into something unhealthy.

Using frightening religious symbolism in this political argument also makes sense because Obama has consistently portrayed his political aims as the great moral cause of our time, one that pits the forces of decency and empathy against the self-serving profiteers of the old guard. His central case for government's existence rests on the notion that the state is society's moral center, the engine of prosperity, and the arbiter of fairness. Obama treats government as a theocrat treats his Church—but he's got an army and the Internal Revenue Service to ensure your participation.

Anyone who stands in the way of Obama's vacuous moral constructs is branded an obstructionist, unpatriotic, a hostage taker, "the enemy," or worse. Those of us who refuse to buy into left-wing orthodoxy remain "uninformed" and, inevitably, "selfish," a bunch of bigoted clods, intellectual buffoons, and moral cripples who got our deserved comeuppance in the 2012 election. If we continue to insist that partisanship is a healthy, organic reflection of differences in a vibrant society—Republicans, after all, still control the House—we can expect to be demonized as remnants of a brutal and obsolete age. Under Obama and his progressive successors, all must submit to the progressive agenda. You saw a bit of this after the election when liberal commentators kept crowing about how the Republican party is a rump party of elderly white males; either the party changes—by which the liberals mean, becomes more progressive—or they gleefully predict it will die.

Progressives are in power, and Obama has treated the political arena as a massive socialist revival meeting. Obama spent four years preaching his own brand of progressive morality: everyone "must" sacrifice. Obama challenged Americans "to find meaning in something greater than themselves," and by that "something greater," he meant government. Every initiative he proposes, every law he signs, is an expansion of the state.

The American political conversation is not what it used to be. We're no longer debating policy, no longer talking about whether government should be merely huge or whether it should be ginormous. We're not really wrangling over what levels of debt or spending are acceptable. We are in a clash for the soul of our country.

And we're losing.

Here are the facts. Obama won reelection convincingly in 2012. There was no theoretical hope-peddling this time around. There was no mystery about what Obama stood for. He had a record of comprehensive economic failure, of divisiveness, of attacks on freedom of religion. He had a record of relentless class warfare, cronyism, incompetence, and stagnation. There were many broken promises. This time around, Barack Obama wasn't bashful about plying the most explicitly left-wing agenda in presidential history—more government, more taxes, more dependency, more bailouts, more regulations—and he won easily. He promised government-run health care, more crony "investments" in proven economic losers, more interference in markets, more coercion, and more redistribution—yet he cruised to victory. He promised these things as the economy sputtered and his foreign policy crumbled.

Conservatives lost, and the prospects are grim.

If you're a conservative, you might be shocked by the statist slogans tossed around at the Democratic National Convention about government being "the only thing that we all belong to." You might be completely scandalized to hear an American president utter the words "you didn't build that," and to argue that private businesses owe their success to a beneficent government.

You might think these statist sentiments are outrageous. But your neighbors? Not so much. We talk about liberty, but many Americans are far less worried about preserving individual freedom and far more attracted to politicians who make promises about what government can do for them.

Things can change to some extent. Political variables are always in motion. A retooled and revamped Republican Party might help. Perhaps a new charismatic leader can better articulate the values of mainstream conservatism. But let's not fool ourselves. There's been a fundamental shift, especially among young people, in how Americans view government's role in society that will be difficult to ever turn around. A Pew Research study conducted after the election found that nearly six in ten of the voters under thirty supported a more expansive role for government in solving problems.

Put it this way: in a post-election poll, Gallup found that more than half of Democrats and left-leaning Americans had a positive view of socialism. Democrats—the majority party in the United States—have a more positive image of the federal government than they do of capitalism. And there is every reason to believe that it will get worse, as Obama works at expanding the power of government, at telling us that government knows best and is the highest calling (and a darn good employer), that government has the answers to all our problems and can take care of us. As recent elections bear out, a large portion of the electorate is happy to embrace this vision.

Feeling depressed? Well, hey, nothing is meant to last forever. With all that's gone on, all the divisive rhetoric, all the political ploys, all the executive abuse, all the hyper-nastiness, one may have forgotten that the Golden Age of Obama dawned with a call to fundamentally remake America. Mission accomplished. If you happen to believe, as I do, that government should be strong, but limited, and that individual freedom is more vital than fairness—guess what? We're screwed. And how.

CHAPTER TWO

FREE STUFF NOW! (SLAVERY LATER)

"Everybody in Cleveland, low minorities, got Obama phone. Keep Obama in president, you know. He gave us a phone...."
—WOMAN AT AN ANTI-ROMNEY RALLY, SEPTEMBER 2012

"The lessons of history, confirmed by the evidence immediately before me, show conclusively that continued dependence upon relief induces a spiritual and moral disintegration fundamentally destructive to the national fibre. To dole out relief in this way is to administer a narcotic, a subtle destroyer of the human spirit. It is inimical to the dictates of sound policy. It is in violation of the traditions of America."
—PRESIDENT FRANKLIN D. ROOSEVELT,
ANNUAL MESSAGE TO CONGRESS, JANUARY 4, 1935

"Freedom is not empowerment. Empowerment is what the Serbs have in Bosnia. Anybody can grab a gun and be empowered. It's not entitlement. An entitlement is what people on welfare get, and how free are they? It's not an endlessly expanding list of rights—the 'right' to education, the 'right' to health care, the 'right' to food and housing. That's not freedom, that's dependency. Those aren't rights, those are the rations of slavery—hay and a barn for human cattle."
—P. J. O'ROURKE, REMARKS AT A
CATO INSTITUTE GALA DINNER, MAY 6, 1993

Sweet Julia

What exactly does the electorate want from its government?

Well, President Barack Obama didn't kick off his reelection bid with a political ad boasting about his administration's success at renewing America's economic superiority—because, frankly, that would have been laughable. And, no, he didn't celebrate the rekindling of American entrepreneurship, because it was contracting rapidly. Neither did Obama lecture us on the "genius" of free enterprise (something he often had alleged to admire during his first term), because that would have been such a transparent sham that even the obsequious media wouldn't have been able to accept it. He didn't crow about the impending boom in green energy production and he certainly didn't brag about anything as piddling as the growth of American living standards, because there was none.

No. There was only one thing he could promise—and he promised plenty of it. Free goodies.

"The Life of Julia"[1] was a small bit of "dependency porn" laid out in cartoon form, a dumbed-down celebration of statism. And what a life it was—starting when she is three years old, Julia's storyline reflects, quite accurately, how things will turn out for many of our unfortunate daughters and granddaughters. It was a reflection of the new reality. Giving and getting free stuff is the moral imperative of the progressive left, the cause that ignites passion in the Obama Age, the reason we have government—it's what makes us moral and free. As Cass Sunstein, one of Obama's favorite technocrats, once wrote: "There is no liberty without dependency."[2]

Julia? Well, you know the drill: The young girl is enrolled in a Head Start program to help get her ready for school because of steps President Obama has taken to improve the program....

Soon enough, Julia can take the SAT because she was trained in the "Race to the Top" program, implemented, yes, by President Obama....

During college, Julia undergoes surgery, which her parent's insurance covers, because Obama guaranteed she could stay on their coverage until she was twenty-six.

Julia then works as a full-time web designer, and thanks to Obamacare, her health insurance is required to cover birth control and preventive care, "letting Julia focus on her work rather than worry about her health" (because children are bad for your health, obviously).

Julia even gives birth to a son named Zachary. There is no father around as far as anyone can tell—and really, who needs some patriarch lording over our every decision, when there are far smarter people up to the task in Washington?

Finally, Julia retires. "After years of contributing to Social Security, she receives monthly benefits that help her retire comfortably, without worrying she'll run out of savings.... This allows her to volunteer at a community garden."

Way to dream, Julia!

So, when it was all said and done, there is 67-year-old Julia—and, if things shake out, you and I—toiling in a community garden in some nondescript, mixed-use, green, urban-ish community in a world where everything is sustainable but a government program. Julia's not going to be one of those bourgeois landholders demanding low taxes. She is perfectly content with her modest lot in life, secure in the knowledge that she has never been too selfish. She has lived a life of partnership with well-intentioned bureaucrats and displayed a lifelong appreciation for their guidance.

Is this what Americans really want? Actually, it is. At least according to recent major elections, enough of the electorate desires that future to make it real. We Americans are bigger fans of cradle-to-grave comfort than we think—much bigger. When we peer into the deeply pathetic life of Julia, we have a better idea of what's in store for many of our own children. When they're old enough, I hope my two daughters won't believe that their success hinges on the charity of others. What I don't want is for them is to be sucked into the self-perpetuating cycle of government dependency. But increasingly, that seems to be the charge of government. This story of an imaginary woman who lives her entire life benefiting from various government programs—paid for by other people's work rather than her own initiative or accomplishments—is emblematic of the entire agenda of the new progressive era. It's an idea that is corroding politics and our morality. Consequently, it will help devastate the economy.

Why would so many Americans believe any differently when everyone in the Democratic Party, the news media, and pop culture is telling them the capitalist system is rigged against their best interests? If this is true, why shouldn't the state guarantee your future? This is how entitlement becomes normalized; it's how the state rectifies the injustices of free markets (which, in their eyes, are the injustices of life in America).

This ideology has festered on the margins of American political thought for a long time, but the Obama administration brought it front and center. The president has more than half the country believing that his is the ideology of progress, when it is the ideology of antiquated early-twentieth-century progressivism. There is nothing new here. If you listen to Obama, dependency is the central argument for government's presence. We *should* depend on government to pave our way through life. Consequently, during Obama's administration, millions of men and women have put control of their destinies in the hands of a massive institution that asks little of them. In fact, come election time, it promises them anything their imaginations can conjure up. The consequences of this unsustainable relationship between the state and its people will be far-reaching—and it is a moral decay as well as an economic one.

Julia's mom wasn't the one who taught her how to interact with her friends, or learn manners, or find self-respect or a moral center. She might never really learn about these things the way you or I did. Mom didn't teach her how to add or multiply or about the birds and the bees. Public schools can teach your children about everything, even sexual behavior—actually, you'll be a lot better off surrendering this task to government, because you're probably too narrow-minded to do it right anyway.

Government schools and Head Start programs are far superior educators to Moms and Dads. Never mind the fact that a 2010 study by the Department of Health and Human Services found that the positive effects of Head Start completely vanish by a child's first year of school.[3] It's the thought that counts, right? And better that government, rather than parents, concentrate on giving a child a "head start." Obama expanded funding for the program by billions.[4]

Who could oppose a program like Head Start, which is about "kids" and "education"? This is part of the progressive narcotic. These days, you simply can't argue against spending billions on "kids" and "education" or anything else that sounds good because if you do you're seen as heartless, as opposed to kids and education, and you might even be part of a Republican Party "war" on kids and education. Progressives always assert that greed drives capitalism, but of course they never see any greed in bureaucrats who relentlessly argue that every failed government program is underfunded.

Head Start is, well, just the start. Julia didn't have to contemplate which career made the most economic sense for her, because the government provided her with student loans regardless. She won't have to worry about health coverage because no matter what choices she makes, it will be provided for her. "Free" birth control and "reproductive health care" will always be available for Julia too. It used to be said that storks delivered babies, but we now know that government has put the storks out of business, both in preventing "unwanted" pregnancies with state-subsidized contraception and abortion, and by stepping in to care for Julia and her child every step of the way from prenatal care to retirement, where, as we know, Social Security is a pillar of the liberal American Dream, an untouchable foundational program of decency—and an example of how the government's well-intentioned intrusions grow to the point of bankruptcy. Social Security was originally intended to supplement the retirement incomes of struggling Americans; it was not intended as a middle class entitlement. But Julia counts on it and Obama plans to "save" it—even if any of us will be lucky to get a one percent return on the money government has stripped from our paychecks. Every step of the way, Obama and big government are there to look after us and make us happy.

Immoral Hazard

If you're old enough, you might remember when your parents didn't let you loaf around at home in your 20s, waiting for the perfect job. You were expected to grow up, leave home, find work, and start your own life. In those days, of course, mooching off government handouts was embarrassing, or even unthinkable, for a 26-year-old. At 26, you held a job and you might have been completely independent and making your way in the world. You might even have been thinking of marriage and supporting a family. You were expected to be an adult.

That was the case even in my day (way back in the 1990s)—and we thought of ourselves as Generation X slackers—lacking the ambition of our parents, but not looking for a life on the dole either. Apparently, we have a different problem with "Generation Y," those born between the 1980s and 1990s, who form a large part of the progressive political voting bloc. The most pervasive accomplishment of "the Millennium Generation"—at least the one we hear about— seems to be moving back home with their parents and demanding goodies. Not all of them, of course. But the shift in generational expectations is indisputable.

Professor Paul Harvey of the University of New Hampshire conducted studies that measure psychological levels of entitlement and narcissism. Lo and behold, he found that members of Generation Y scored 25 percent higher than respondents aged 40–60 and 50 percent higher than those over 61.[5] Gen-Yers, in fact, were twice as apt to rank in the top 20 percent—the "highly entitled range"—as someone between 40 and 60. They were four times more likely to expect things from others than a crabby old coot on a pension. Professor Harvey believes that Gen-Yers have a "very inflated sense of self" and "unrealistic expectations," which naturally lead to "chronic disappointment." That makes them the perfect demographic to support Barack Obama, who caters to their inherent sense of entitlement and to the injustice they now—after years of cultural propaganda—perceive in a free market system that, among other fresh hells, requires them to pay for their own contraception.

According to the University of Minnesota's Population Center, after using data from the Census Bureau's Current Population Survey, the number of 26-year-olds living with their parents jumped almost 46 percent over the past few years; the number of 18- to 30-year-olds living with their parents grew by 21 million.[6] A Pew poll found that as many as four in ten adults between the ages of 18 and 34 had moved back in with their folks.[7] For those who believe this is all a function of a bad economy, think again. We've never seen anything like it. Not in the Great Depression, not ever. It's a matter of attitude, not economic necessity.

"I'm 26 years old and haven't grown up yet," says one Mr. Sanchez to a Bloomberg reporter exploring the implications of this trend. "I've become so comfortable with the lifestyle I've been living." I bet you have. Parents and grandparents increasingly foot the bills for twenty-somethings who are happy to lounge their way through an extended adolescence. A recent AARP survey of grandparents found that grandpa and grandma weren't sneaking the grandkids the odd candy bar anymore; in many cases, they were helping with their grandchildren's educational expenses (53 percent), everyday living expenses (37 percent), and even their medical or dental expenses (23 percent).[8] A student loan and a few checks from mom and dad and grandma and grandpa can extend your life of communications studies and keg parties at Mega-State University—one day fulfilling your promise and attaining that taxpayer-supported professorship at the school. Getting something for nothing is the new normal, because after all, Gen-Yers deserve it; they feel entitled to this "lifestyle" of having everything taken care of for them.

At the Republican National Convention in 2012, Paul Ryan had a nightmare vision, which is today's reality, of young adults destined to "live out their twenties in their childhood bedrooms, staring up at fading Obama posters and wondering when they can move out and get going with life." Only they might not be thinking of moving out. The president of the United States, after all, boasts about how his greatest achievement, Obamacare, has put 3.1 million "young" Americans under age twenty-six on government-impelled health insurance. Any politician that might suggest we need to undo this bit of budding paternalism will be accused of denying health care to millions of vulnerable "children." And Americans, apparently, have never been more childlike.

A Nation of Unemployed Students

One of the very few policy battles being won—slowly—by the nation's free-market activists is the expansion of school choice. Among African Americans and Latinos—and others who have experienced the tragic failure of government-run inner-city schools up close and personal—there has been a rise in popularity of charter schools, magnet schools, and various other choices in public schools. Many of these districts have become more competitive and more diverse, and even liberal parents regularly turn to alternatives in education. More vitally, it gives those who want to escape state-run incompetence (although they'd never put it that way) a chance to partake in a dynamic competitive market. Unless courts and taxpayer-funded teachers' unions stop it, a full-blown voucher system for grade school education can't be far away. When it comes to a college education, however, we're headed in the opposite direction.

Not long ago, a liberal acquaintance of mine was lecturing me (because that's what liberal acquaintances tend to do best) on how secondary education is "free" in nearly every civilized country but ours. Why doesn't America, he queried, provide this basic right to all its citizens?

Let's start with the obvious: college used to be about having the chance to earn your way through college and better yourself. Now college is an entitlement with government-subsidized tuition and government loans covering the cost. At the risk of sounding like a prehistoric troglodyte, why should you or I be on the hook to pay for Julia's course work in the Science of Harry Potter at Maryland's Frostburg University or in Queer Musicology at UCLA or in Cyberfeminism at Cornell (all real courses, by the way)? The fact is, a lot of what goes on at our colleges is a joke funded by the taxpayers, and a means of providing employment for otherwise unemployable "academics," not to mention a way for our "children" to spend a few more years removed from adult responsibilities until they are properly credentialed for middle class life—which is how most parents these days think of college. But a college education isn't always a good thing or a good return on a student's (or a parent's or a grandparent's or a taxpayer's) investment. A lot of it depends on what you study, and where. The idea that college is a surefire way to achieve economic success is bogus. Wikipedia has a page devoted to college dropout billionaires (the list includes high tech entrepreneurs like Steve Jobs, Mark Zuckerberg, and Bill Gates). But politicians like Obama peddle the idea of college as an investment in our future (by the taxpayers of course), a sort of economic panacea and de facto "right" for all, because it gives politicians another chance to be in favor of "education," it enlarges the managerial and bureaucratic state, and even because it marinades students in another few years of liberal indoctrination under progressive professors. But as Boyce Watkins, a professor of finance at Syracuse University, told NPR, a college education without an economic direction and incentive isn't always helpful:[9]

You know, when I went to college, I didn't think of college as a luxury item as some of my friends did. I thought of it as a necessity. Which meant that I was going to college to advance my career, to get an opportunity to actually control my economic future. So I didn't go to college and major in anthropology and philosophy. I went to college and I majored in business because I wanted to get a job. Now, when you have students who are going to college for economic advancement and they chose majors that don't fit that particular objective and then take a lot of debt on in the process, then, you know, you have to ask them, well, Did you plan it all the way through when you ended up with an outcome that you didn't quite expect? So I think that going to college is certainly important. I applaud the president's move to get everyone to go to college, but I think that we have to be very intelligent about what we expect to get out of our education.

In a widely discussed 2012 *Newsweek* piece by Megan McArdle titled, "Is College a Lousy Investment?," Richard Vedder, an economics professor who heads the Center for College Affordability and Productivity at Ohio University, explained, "I look at the data, and I see college costs rising faster than inflation up to the mid-1980s by 1 percent a year. Now I see them rising 3 to 4 percent a year over inflation. What has happened? The federal government has started dropping money out of airplanes." Vedder argues that prices have really taken off since government aid has increased and subsidized loans have become widely available. In other words, government has made college more expensive, which obviously benefits the schools more than the students. It's the schools that have driven educational prices artificially high because there are hundreds of millions of government dollars pouring into the market. As economist Bryan Caplan said, "It's a giant waste of resources that will continue as long as the subsidies continue."[10]

When Congress instituted assistance for low-income families to go to college through federal grants in 1965 (what later became "Pell grants"), they weren't, as far as we can tell from the record, looking to hand out loans to everyone, but rather to help students from poor families get an education that they might not otherwise be able to afford. These programs, like so many other well-intentioned programs, might not work out as planned, but the intent is understandable. The result, however, is a spigot that can't easily be turned off. As *American* magazine pointed out, in the 2009–2010 school year, 7.7 million students received $28.2 billion in Pell grants, which never have to be repaid. The maximum size of Pell grants to individual students increases every year, and the stipends are available to anyone who wants them as long as you are somewhere near the American poverty level.[11] They have, in effect, become a "right."

That's certainly Obama's view. Campaigning in 2012, he alleged, "In America, higher education cannot be a luxury; it's an economic imperative that every family must be able to afford."[12] In another speech, Obama explained that "Michelle and I, we've been in your shoes," and "we only finished paying off our student loans off [sic] about eight years ago. That wasn't that long ago. And that wasn't easy—especially because when we had Malia and Sasha, we're supposed to be saving up for their college educations, and we're still paying off our college educations."[13]

It wasn't easy, but was it worth it, Mr. President of *the United States of America*? I think yes.

It is true that we've created a job market where a college degree is sometimes overvalued and at other times a necessity. But President Obama has shifted the public debate from the idea that college should be accessible to all Americans who are academically qualified and can afford it to the idea that college should appear to be cheap—subsidized through direct government funding, grants, and loans—and for everybody—even if in reality government-financed distortions of the market make a college education far more expensive than it should be, and expanding enrollment only means expanding the number of the indebted.

There is a vital difference. If you have to invest in your own future, you're likely to make a thoughtful decision; you don't want to waste money you've worked hard to earn. You'll think about what course of study, and what college, might give you the best return on your investment. You might even decide that rather than attending college you'd be better off starting your own business. But government grants, subsidies, and loans mean that fewer and fewer young people think this way about their future. College is simply another right to which they are entitled.

During the 2012 campaign, Obama tried to motivate young voters by asking Congress to pass legislation that would set student loan repayments at artificially low interest rates or forgive them altogether. This kind of price fixing creates an economic bubble that will one day pop. With the election fast approaching, he leapfrogged the democratic process and began nationalizing student loans through an executive order, allowing student borrowers with direct government loans and government-backed private loans to consolidate balances, limiting student loan payments to 10 percent of a graduate's income, and forgiving debt still outstanding after twenty years.[14] In the end, the order didn't do much (saving students around $10 a month), except to make students who had actually paid off their loans feel like suckers (this seems to be the government way, punishing the responsible and rewarding the improvident), but he did raise expectations among the young that student loans will no longer be the burden they seem. The message was clear, though. It's perhaps no surprise that according to national exit polling from CNN, 59 percent of 18- to 29-year olds voted for Obama.[15] He worked to buy their votes, and he succeeded.

While twenty-somethings might believe big government involvement is a positive development, forgiving their loans and entitling them to more free stuff, what government is really doing is creating a moral hazard that has the potential to lead to future structural unemployment—with the government subsidizing a mismatch between demand in the labor market and the skills of workers. If you can't pay back your loan because your job doesn't pay enough, you don't have the right job or the right education. A Rasmussen poll found that only 21 percent of adults think the federal government should forgive the nearly $1 trillion in loans it made or guaranteed to help students pay for a college education.[16] But how far away can a movement for a complete government bailout of student loans be? And once initiated, or led by, Obama, who thinks that Congress will stand in the way? Who would want to be painted as "anti-education"?

Senator Lamar Alexander, former secretary of education, told *National Review* that President Obama's new policies on the federal student loan program were a "Soviet-style" takeover, "truly brazen," and the "most underreported big-Washington takeover" in the history of the nation. "Up to now, 15 out of 19 million student loans were private loans, backed by the government. Now we're going to borrow half-a-trillion from China to pay for billions in new loans. Not only will this add to the debt, but in the middle of a recession, this will throw 31,000 Americans working at community banks and non-profit lenders out of work."[17] Or as the *Wall Street Journal* editorial board put it, the U.S. Department of Education wants to be the "exclusive banker to America's college students."[18]

There is no way back. Once government has absolved loans and artificially pushed down interest rates, there is no politician on earth who will run to raise rates and make higher education "more expensive"—and if they did, they probably wouldn't be elected anyway. In effect, we are in the process of transforming the system into something that resembles public schools—one system for the masses and a private system for those who can afford it.

Transforming college into a guaranteed dependency program (because soon enough we'll be forgiving loans as we forgive mortgages, so that someone else pays for them) only ensures that millions of young people will earn degrees that don't correspond to productive and prosperous private sector jobs; in the process, it will boost America's already massive debt. It also means that the government will increase its influence over private schools, making them ever more dependent on subsidies, grants, and loans. That's just the way progressives like it.

No Worries, We've Got You—and You and You and You and You—Covered

When the end finally comes—when reliance on government finally outstrips private-sector prosperity—a terrible choice will confront us: either we slash the government on which we've become dependent (an unlikely scenario), or we accept a grimmer future of limited expectations. It appears that many Americans have already made that choice.

A recent Rasmussen Reports poll found that a mere 14 percent of American adults believe today's children will enjoy a better life than their parents did—an all-time low for that question.[19] Americans are increasingly skeptical about the American Dream. Only 28 percent believe that anyone can work hard and get rich in the United States. According to an Associated Press-Viacom poll, a majority of Americans aged 18 to 24 expect it will be tougher for them to buy a house and save for retirement than it was for their parents.[20] And a Gallup poll discovered that the percentage of Americans who believe they'll be worse off in four years has more than doubled since Obama was first inaugurated as president.[21] Yet the American people reelected him anyway.

It's true that many people don't blame Obama for the current hard economic times. (Obama certainly doesn't blame himself; he spent four years and the campaign blaming his predecessor.) But in 2012 the American people had a choice between two starkly different (at least in theory) futures: one based on a state-led economy and one that tried to steer back towards America's free-market model. The voters chose the candidate of bigger government. It's hard not to come to the conclusion that the American electorate of today is increasingly willing to trade freedom and prosperity for government insurance and dependency. Guaranteed entitlement, even at the cost of declining standards of living, seems easier, safer, and more equitable. It seems like a better bet than a free economy that has winners and losers and that offers no guarantees.

In the 1980s, around 30 percent of American households received some form of welfare. In the 1990s, it rose to 35 percent.[22] In the Obama era, it has leapt to nearly 50 percent, according to a study conducted by the *Wall Street Journal*.[23] That's much higher than the

16 percent of Americans who are estimated to live in poverty and a shocking reversal of the traditional American belief in self-reliance. According to the Bureau of Economic Analysis, in 1960 taxpayers spent $24 billion (adjusted for inflation) on entitlement programs. By the middle of Obama's first term that aid had multiplied 100 times. Even when accounting for population growth and inflation, spending on entitlement increased around 725 percent.[24]

Last year, a report from the independent Congressional Research Service found that welfare was now the single largest federal expense—greater than Social Security, Medicare, and national defense—with combined state and federal spending on welfare programs topping $1 trillion in 2011. When the group put together its overview of cumulative means-tested federal welfare spending in the United States, it found that there were more than eighty-three overlapping programs, exactly the kind of efficiency we expect from government but a disaster for Americans. Federal spending on these programs came to around $746 billion and state spending required for participation cost around $283 billion.[25] For some context, in 2011, the annual budget expenditure for Social Security was $725 billion, Medicare was $480 billion, and non-war defense was $540 billion.

And these programs always swell. In 1960, for example, around 455,000 workers were receiving disability payments from the government. The percentage of the "economically active" population between the ages of 18–64 getting disability benefits was 0.65 percent. By 2011, 8,600,000 workers were receiving disability payments from the government. The percentage of the "economically active" population between the ages of 18–64 years old getting disability benefits was 5.6 percent. In 1948, 89 percent of men age 20 and over were in the workforce. By 2011, only 73 percent were. In this nation, we've had increasingly less physically demanding jobs and far better medical care, so that number should be growing, not shrinking.[26]

Every year the conservative Heritage Foundation puts together a study called the Index of Dependence on Government, and every year under Obama, the dependence rate has gone up. Over four years it has gone up nearly a third (by 31.73 percent). It's going to get worse, because, as the Heritage report warns, "there are the 78 million baby boomers who have begun to head into retirement. Further whittling the taxpayer rolls, many are projected to be substantially if not entirely dependent on Social Security and Medicare, further exacerbating the federal spending crisis that currently exists."[27]

If the goal of the welfare state is to help the poor escape poverty, it is manifestly not working. After half a century of waging a War on Poverty through an ever-expanding list of government programs, more than 46 million Americans still qualify as poor, according to the 2010 Census.[28] In 2008, 13.2 percent of the population was living in poverty; that number rose to 14.3 percent in 2009[29] and to more than 16 percent in 2012.[30] A 2012 update of the Census data pegged the number of poor Americans at nearly 50 million.[31] But the dirty little secret of all this of course is that the federal government—its bureaucrats, its liberal political patrons—has a vested interest in ever-expanding welfare rolls. The business of big government is government: the more of it, the better. That's the whole point.

The great federal welfare trough is all interconnected. Few Americans probably know that food stamps (now called the Supplemental Nutrition Assistance Program, or SNAP) are part of the Farm Bill. Today, one in seven Americans use them and the number is growing.[32] Food stamps have little to do directly with food or nutrition (as the "we accept food stamps" sign outside 7-11 could probably tell you), and are essentially cash handouts—and it's a lot of cash. Between 2001 and October 2011 the number of people receiving food stamps leapt from 17.3 million to an astonishing 46.2 million.[33] The 10-year budget for food stamps is projected to reach nearly $800 billion.[34] The Department of Agriculture is, in essence, a welfare department of its own. Around 80 percent of the spending authorized by the "Farm Bill" goes to food stamps.

Food stamps have been one of Obama's singular successes at creating government dependency. He even made expanding the program part of his "stimulus" plan. By the end of 2012 the number of people on food stamps was greater than the entire population of California or Australia,[35] and the Obama administration is looking to make the number of food stamp dependents even bigger. The U.S. Department of Agriculture spent around $3 million on a series of ads imploring people to find out if they too were eligible.[36] "Millions of low-income people are not accessing the nutrition benefits for which they qualify," notes a USDA flyer addressing "myths" about government assistance. "To be effective, it is important that our national and local outreach efforts counter myths about SNAP among those who think they are not eligible or have beliefs that discourage them from enrolling."[37]

"Beliefs that discourage them from enrolling" no doubt include beliefs that used to characterize what it meant to be an American: pride, resourcefulness, independence, self-sufficiency, and personal responsibility. It wasn't so long ago that people shied away from receiving charity; it was a source of shame. If they were truly hard up, they would try to find help from their extended family or their local church. Accepting government handouts was a last resort. Now it is a right, and the goal of government is not to encourage self-reliance but to make poverty more comfortable. Even worse, it is to balkanize our country into different government-dependent clients.

This was inadvertently revealed when former Speaker of the House Newt Gingrich called President Obama the "food stamp president."[38] Liberals jumped all over Gingrich, calling him—what else?—a racist. But Gingrich aptly remarked that the real racists were those who assumed that food stamps were just for blacks.[39] "If you in fact talk openly and honestly about the failure of liberal institutions and the way they hurt the poor, there comes a sudden frenzied herd of people running over screaming racism, racism," Gingrich explained.

I would argue that it is even more thoughtless—and the consequences more harmful to minorities—to craft programs that funnel healthy men and women into state-run serfdom. And if racism is what liberals are looking for, the most tragic comment on food stamps came from another former Speaker of the House. In 2011, speaking at Jesse Jackson's Rainbow PUSH Coalition, House Democratic Leader Nancy Pelosi said that Gingrich's comment that Obama was the "Food Stamp President" was a "badge of honor."[40] After all, what could be a greater accomplishment than putting more people on the dole? It shows that Pelosi and Obama and the Democratic Party care about the poor; they care so much that they'd like to take care of them forever, with what is becoming almost an inheritance of state-based state assistance. And of course those who pat themselves on the back for fostering this immoral class system like to think they deserve all the votes of the dependent class.

There are only two ways to look at Pelosi's "badge of honor" remarks. Either she's an authoritarian who believes that greater dependence on government is for the better, or she's a nihilist who simply doesn't care that dependency leads to stunted lives. Then again, maybe she's both.

Obama seems to be both, because his administration actually rolled back one of the most successful—and rare—bipartisan efforts in modern political history: the Clinton administration's celebrated legislative accomplishment of welfare reform. Not surprisingly, Obama opposed welfare reform in 1996,[41] as did about half of the Democrats in Congress. With a push from the conservative, Republican-majority Congress, Bill Clinton promised to "end welfare as we know it."[42] At the 1996 bill signing he said, "Today, we have an historic opportunity to make welfare what it was meant to be, a second chance, not a way of life."[43] Over the next four years, caseloads fell by more than half, from 12.6 million to 5.9 million,[44] and the welfare rolls kept dropping, albeit at a slower pace, after that, with most of the former welfare recipients finding jobs. But in July 2012, Obama's Department of Health and Human Services gutted the work requirements that helped so many get off the rolls.[45] When the Romney campaign called them out, the administration went on the offensive. Bill Clinton called the charge that the president had undone his major achievement "a real doozy."[46] Obama Press Secretary Jay Carney claimed that the charge was "categorically false" and "blatantly dishonest."[47] The *New York Times*, in an editorial titled "Mr. Romney Hits Bottom on Welfare," mixed it up a bit, calling the accusation "blatantly false."[48]

But, as it turns out, the Obama administration did indeed waive the federally mandated work requirement and let states set their own standards. Robert Rector, who helped draft the 1996 legislation, affirmed that the Obama administration had negated the law, which explicitly prohibited waivers on work requirements.[49] The Government Accountability Office agreed and said the Obama administration had overstepped its authority.[50] It did so not only by eliminating work requirements but also by altering the metrics used to measure success. The welfare reform law barred welfare programs from measuring success as bureaucrats like to do: in terms of increasing caseloads. So the Obama administration has caved in to the bureaucrats: the more cases you have the more successful you are. Bigger government is better government. Dependence on government is now the goal.

Many Americans need assistance, granted, but Democrats have created a political environment where any person pointing out facts about welfare spending that fails to adhere to the narrative that welfare is a moral necessity is going to be smeared. The fact of the matter is that someone is abusing the system. Probably a lot of "someones." The Republican side of the Senate Budget Committee, for instance, found that welfare spending per day per household in poverty adds up to about $168. This is higher than the $137 median income per day of the average American. Welfare spending per hour per household in poverty is $30.60. That is also higher than the $25.03 median income per hour. Based on data from the Congressional Research Service, wrote the Senate Budget Committee, "cumulative spending on means-tested federal welfare programs, if converted into cash, would equal $167.65 per day per household living below the poverty level. By comparison, the median household income in 2011 of $50,054 equals $137.13 per day. Additionally, spending on federal welfare benefits, if converted into cash payments, equals enough to provide $30.60 per hour, 40 hours per week, to each household living below poverty."[51] In another rather amazing catch by Wyatt Emerich of the *Cleveland Current*, using the "benefits calculators" of various welfare programs, he comes to the rather persuasive conclusion that "a one-parent family of three making $14,500 a year (minimum wage) has more disposable income than a family making $60,000 a year."[52]

War Is Peace. Freedom Is Slavery.
Giving Is Taking.

This kind of massive entitlement society doesn't just show up on our doorsteps. More than any one program—although there are plenty to talk about—the most destructive and consequential part of the mounting dependency state is the way it distorts words, ideas, and how we think about government.

Dependency dooms us by making us believe we're all victims. The deck, liberals like to argue, is stacked against us. If you're a woman, or black, or poor, or Latino, or gay, or just about anyone who isn't a rich white heterosexual guy driving a Beemer, life is a total bitch. In recent years, especially since the Great Recession hit, the middle class—despite living better collective lives than anyone the world has ever known—has also somehow attained a victim status.

When the recessionary times took hold (the worst economic disaster since the Vandals sacked Rome, the president would have you believe), we were bombarded by chilling tales of how the wealthy vampire class sucked all the capital from the market, denied you your car loan, drained your 401ks, and made your wife grouchy. If you couldn't pay your mortgage, then someone had obviously bamboozled you into taking that loan. Free will, after all, is a myth. And since we've been hoodwinked, we've gotta devise ways to redistribute back to the people what the plutocrats stole from the rest of us. That's the economic mythology peddled by progressives and by the president—a brand of thinking once confined to college campuses and now prevalent among even supposedly moderate Democrats.

Pretending we are all victims of duplicitous Wall Street bankers and the wealthy "1 percent" is what drives progressive economic politics. Obama and his allies have used this fable to conflate socialism with "fairness." Obama himself put it that way, more or less: "I want to live in a society that's fair"—meaning, of course, that he doesn't live in one now.[53] The society he wants is one where we "spread the wealth around;" where "you didn't build that" business of yours, government did; and where wealth is finite and the government needs to take a bigger role in redistributing it.

Bertrand Russell once observed that "advocates of capitalism are very apt to appeal to the sacred principles of liberty, which are embodied in one maxim: The fortunate must not be restrained in the exercise of tyranny over the unfortunate."[54] That seems to be Obama's view of his ideological opponents—they are nothing but shills for the wealthy. He and his team hit upon this theme incessantly during the 2012 election campaign. In a 2012 speech in Osawatomie, Kansas, Obama dismissed free market capitalism as a "simple theory," which "fits well on a bumper sticker. But here's the problem: it doesn't work." Obama tried to wrap himself in the mantle of Theodore Roosevelt, saying that in Roosevelt's time, "some people thought massive inequality and exploitation was just the price of progress.... But Roosevelt also knew that the free market has never been a free license to take whatever you want from whoever you can."[55] Actually, the people who believe they have a free license to take whatever they want from whomever they can are Obama and the Democrats. That's how they "spread the wealth around." The free market, on the other hand, is not about "taking" wealth, it's about creating wealth; it isn't about "taking" things, it's about creating things; there's no coercion involved in the free market, as there always is in government action; it's about free trade.

Obama went on to say that the middle class struggle to find a decent life is the "defining issue of our time" and claimed that Americans "rightly" suppose that the economy is rigged against their best interests. Those interests are better served, apparently, by the unions, ramped up government spending and regulation, and government-directed (or crony) capitalism.

As we neared Election Day, the president said, "We don't believe that anybody is entitled to success in this country," a rather bizarre inversion of the classic American ideal that anyone can attain success through hard work. Instead of that hopeful message, Obama implied that some people don't deserve the success they have. If you believe, as Obama apparently does, that wealth is finite, it's not a leap to presume that the wealthy gained their wealth by stealing it, by taking more than their fair share from some communal wealth pile. What we see as government dependency, he sees as redressing an injustice, which is why growing welfare rolls are a positive and not a negative.

In Obama's America, except for the wealthiest 1 percent, we're all victims.

Luckily, government is here, and Obama is here, to make us happy and to help us. After Obama's 2008 victory, one excited fan famously claimed that Obama's election "was the most memorable time of my life. It was a touching moment. Because I never thought this day would ever happen. I won't have to worry about putting gas in my car. I won't have to worry about paying my mortgage. You know, if I help him, he's gonna help me."

That's what liberal politicians had been telling her, and she believed it. Obama was the politician, after all, who in his June 3, 2008, speech accepting the nomination of the Democratic Party for president, said that "this was the moment when we began to provide care for the sick and good jobs to the jobless; this was the moment when the rise of the oceans began to slow and our planet began to heal." Obama is one powerful politician. And in his bag of gifts, there is something for everyone: condoms for college kids; pills for women; dollars for the poor; federal funds, in fact, for just about everybody except angry white working-age non-unionized self-reliant hetero-sexual males, who, as liberal reporters gleefully crowed after the 2012 presidential election, no longer have enough votes to elect anyone.

Obama-era politics is the politics of happiness, of government that helps you do anything you want and that ensures that someone else pays for it. This era sees politics and government as primary—as more fundamental than businesses or churches or volunteer organi-zations or even the family. That woman who thought Obama's elec-tion "was the most memorable time of my life" had a child with her. The child played second fiddle to Obama. So did the rule of law and the Constitution, which says nothing about freeing people from their mortgage payments. The view that happiness and freedom come from government is not a view the Founders would have known or endorsed. They put limitations on government so men would be free, so they could pursue happiness. Now happiness comes from the government.

"If you are willing to work hard you should be able to find a good job," Obama said during a campaign event in 2012. "If you're meeting your responsibilities, you should be able to own a home, maybe start a business."[56] And government is there to make sure it happens. Gone, apparently, is the idea that a person who meets his responsibilities is simply performing at the most basic level of an adult; gone is the idea that it would be absurd for a president to promise a responsible adult whatever he wants. It was David Cameron, prime minister of the United Kingdom, and a man doing an outstanding job of managing Britain's own decline, who explained that it was "time we admitted that there's more to life than money and it's time we focused not just on GDP but on GWB—general wellbeing."[57] He added: "Wellbeing can't be measured by money or traded in markets. It's about the beauty of our surroundings, the quality of our culture and, above all, the strength of our relationships. Improving our society's sense of wellbeing is, I believe, the central political challenge of our times."

As the English might say, rubbish.

David Cameron has absolutely no clue what makes any of us happy. My happiness can't be gauged by the size of my bank account, but neither can it be measured by a government bureaucrat. Maybe I live to eat Twinkies, take Tequila shots, and read trashy romance novels. How would Cameron calculate my happiness? The goal of government (in this country, at least) is to create an environment of law and order where contracts are kept and people are free to voluntarily engage in trade and in things that make them happy.

But government definitely wants to get into the happiness business. During the first year of the European recession, Nicolas Sarkozy, then president of France, commissioned two Nobel prize-winning liberal economists, Joseph Stiglitz and Amartya Sen, to investigate how a rising gross domestic product might actually hinder work-life balance and happiness as the administration defined it. Well, as long as we weren't looking for a predetermined answer, right? Or in other words, let's prove that even though the economy is plummeting, it doesn't matter because there are more important things than money.

Social scientists have done plenty of research on happiness in modern society, and in fact President Obama gave senior government positions to three happiness scholars (technocrats who think nothing of coercion): Betsey Stevenson, Alan Krueger, and Cass Sunstein. The result? Americans are about as unhappy as they've ever been in modern times. At least, that's what the recent Gallup-Healthways Well-Being Index shows.[58] Who would have thought that a deep recession, a massive increase in government dependency, and a future of crushing national debt could be so depressing?

When it comes to government, Americans suffer from cognitive dissonance. A recent ABC News/*Washington Post* poll found that 56 percent of Americans preferred smaller government even if it meant fewer government services—this, despite voting for a president who has dramatically expanded government and advocates expanding it even further.[59] Poll after poll reaffirms that most Americans still believe, at least in theory, in the idea of limited, constitutional government—although they might not vote that way. The rational explanation for this phenomenon is that most Americans still understand our nation's founding ideals, even if they pull the voting lever based on other, more immediate, concerns, feelings, or fears. That's just life, although the left, of course, senses hypocrisy, because the left wants to undo those founding ideals entirely.

A 2008 Cornell Survey Research Institute poll was one celebrated instance of the left trying to expose Americans who hold traditional views of the state as hypocrites. It asked 1,400 people if they had "ever used a government social program." Fifty-seven percent said "no." Pollees were then asked if they had partaken from any in a long list of federal programs, including Social Security, unemployment insurance, interest deduction, and student loans. Many, of course, said yes. Aha!

"Americans often fail to recognize government's role in society even if they have experienced it in their own lives," Suzanne Mettler, professor of government at Cornell, wrote in the *New York Times* regarding the study's findings. "That is because so much of what government does today is largely invisible."[60]

There is of course a different way of looking at it. To start, most conservative-minded Americans are not anarchists. They might still use the post office; their children might enlist in the armed forces; they might have city-supplied water; and they might even believe there is a role for a limited welfare state. Paul Ryan and Mitt Romney, after all, had their own plans to save Social Security and Medicare. Second, there was a marked difference in the responses of conservatives and liberals in the poll. Respondents who self-identified as "extremely liberal" were 20 percentage points more likely to acknowledge using a government program than someone who self-identified as "extremely conservative," even if the "extreme conservative" did in fact use the same number of programs. Mettler pointed out "those who believed that the nation spent too much on welfare were less likely to admit that they had used a 'government social program,' perhaps because that term had pejorative connotations."

And, yes, she wrote this like it was a bad thing, because of course mooching off government (that is, taxpayers) is now the American way.

But the Cornell study also failed to differentiate between tax cuts, which in liberal fashion were treated as government handouts, and "government social programs," that rely on coercive extractions of taxpayer dollars. A conservative who accepts a mortgage interest deduction, however, isn't a dependent of the federal government the way a recipient of food stamps is; and a conservative congressman who opposes stimulus spending and then, when the stimulus bill is passed, fights to get some of the money for his state, is only trying to get back some of the taxpayers' dollars that have already been marked for spending. That doesn't make him a hypocrite or someone who "benefits" from big government. It makes him a realist. How many liberals, by the way, have elected to skip "benefitting" from Republican-passed tax cuts?

When a retired Tea Party activist carries a sign that reads, "Don't Let Government Touch My Medicare," liberals laugh. But the activist has already paid into a state-impelled program, and whether he wanted it or not, the liberals made a deal with him. In 1965, Congress created Medicare under Title XVIII of the Social Security Act to provide health insurance to people age sixty-five and older, regardless of income or medical history. Everyone has to pay into it whether they like the idea or not. We're hooked. You can't really blame him for wanting to get something out of all the money the state took from him.

The fact is, Social Security and Medicare aren't "government social programs," they are "coerced government social programs." Americans may like them or they may prefer free-market alternatives, but we no longer have any say in opting out—and liberals will fight to keep these programs coercive. These programs are now embedded in our lives—we pay into them and plan our lives around them. The idea that the government provides Social Security and health care insurance is not a debatable position; it is a truth. Republicans will argue at the margins over how to reform the system, but in the end there's no undoing it. If conservatives use these programs it is only because they have no choice.

The Cornell study claims that an interest deduction in your taxes is a government benefit. That is to assume—as liberals seem to do, knowingly or not—that the baseline for taxation is 100 percent of all your income, and that anything government leaves you should be considered a big favor. It's hard to imagine an assumption more at odds with the principles under which our nation was founded.

But in the Obama era, old American ideals were consistently turned on their heads.

Think, for example, of how Obama—and nearly the entire media—always made sure to discuss the "cost" of allowing Bush-era tax rates to remain as they were, as if Washington had first dibs on your money. Obama often claimed that the country could not afford the "cost" of these tax cuts instituted a decade ago. We (as in the non-wealthy) supposedly "pay" for this lower rate of taxation. But the only thing we really pay for is government spending (or "investment" as the liberals like to call it). In no way do we have to "pay for" money the Internal Revenue Service doesn't collect, unless the assumption is that we are all wards of the state who suffer when money is held privately. Guess what the Obamacrats apparently believe? Whenever President Obama was selling his dependency moralism—which he almost always is—he would refer to it as the "basic social compact."[61] Isn't it about time we shared responsibility, he would say, and kick in our share for the extraordinary benefits provided to us by Washington? By "all" of us, of course, he allegedly meant folks who make more money than we do. He was, in short, appealing to envy and greed.

In one of his speeches on the fiscal cliff crisis, Obama, without even breaking out into fits of laughter, said that Americans must "reduce spending in the tax code." This mystifying phrase, I came to discover after a thorough investigation, translates to this: "Hey, let's tax the rich because everyone hates those bastards anyway." Here the president also explained that your earnings, if you manage to accumulate enough profit, belong by default to the IRS. Keeping too much of your money, as Obama points out, is tantamount to taking it from Washington and thus from those who really need it.

Under Obama, even the meaning of freedom is being distorted through the bait and switch of "positive rights," which the Obama administration moralistically pledges to enforce. In the eyes of an increasing number of liberals, condoms, abortions, health care, salubrious foods, housing, and countless other things, should—if there is any decency in this nation—be a positive right. If people depend on something it should be provided for them. If conservatives think it is up to individuals to provide these things for themselves, they are obviously waging war on women, the poor, and every other group whose needs and desires liberals think should be subsidized.

Here is how the vice president of the United States, Joe Biden, put it on the campaign trial in 2012:[62]

> I want to make this clear so there [is] no misunderstanding anybody. I got a daughter, lost a daughter, got four grand-daughters, and Barack has two daughters. We are abso-lutely—this is to our core—my daughter, and my granddaughters and Barack's daughters are entitled to every single solitary operation! Every single solitary oper-ation!

It's all free, free, free. Sort of. And if it's free—that is, provided by the taxpayer—and somehow we're not getting it, then someone is denying us access to our positive rights. So if a company or an orga-nization—the Catholic Church, for instance—fails to offer birth control to its employees on the ludicrous grounds that this is immoral, it is in actuality denying women access to reproductive health care. So, if you are an observant Catholic, the state not only coerces you out of your money, it coerces you out of your constitu-tional right to freedom of conscience. But of course since most of us in Obama's America are not observant Catholics, what do we care? We'd rather have free morning-after pills than defend the First Amendment.

There's also the more mundane issue that no one in public life advocated pulling contraception out of drug stores, out of doctor's offices, or anywhere else. Not only is contraception cheap, it's widely available. But if government isn't providing it for "free," well.... As I type these words, I have a Democratic Party web page open and it

reads: "REPUBLICANS RESTRICTING ACCESS TO CONTRACEP-
TION."[63] (That irritating capitalization is theirs.) They are "restricting" access by saying that maybe the taxpayer shouldn't have to
subsidize it all the time.

This liberal inversion of the idea of rights and freedoms isn't
exactly new. The left has long argued that there is no freedom for
the poor in a free market because if you lack the ability to purchase
a house, or a car, or a phone, or Internet access, you are in fact being
denied these services and products by the people who have them.
The activist Sandra Fluke famously embodied this philosophy during the 2012 election campaign when she testified against religious
institutions that refused to pay for students' contraception. (She was
a law student at Georgetown, a Catholic school.) Fluke is what
qualifies as a hero in the Entitlement Age—her reputation built on
one thing alone: demanding others pay for her activities. Fluke,
despite reports from the media, was not first and foremost a wom-
en's rights activist; she was, first and foremost, an activist for free
stuff.

Fluke also actively campaigned against the First Amendment. Just
ask the more than forty Catholic organizations—the Catholic University of America, the University of Notre Dame, the archdioceses
of New York and Washington, and so on—that filed suit against
Obamacare's contraception mandate. The Constitution guarantees
the right to the free exercise of religion, a right of conscience. But
when the "positive right" to contraception that Obamacare offers
comes into conflict with the constitutional rights to freedom of religion and freedom of conscience, guess who wins? Freedom loses.
Freedom is a one-way street.

Actually, the arguments for the contraception mandate offer us a
new definition of freedom.

At some point, contraception was transformed—in the views of many people—from a useful way to avoid an unwanted pregnancy into a moral, societal imperative that must be mandated, lest we abandon our daughters, science, decency, public health, "choice," and "freedom." Biden once claimed that this debate is about "the right of women to decide for themselves, whether or not they want to use contraception."[64] But that wasn't the case at all. The issue was why the federal government thought it had the right to determine what kind of health insurance you can buy. A woman could walk down the street and decide whether to buy contraception—even before Obama was president!—but she was apparently not entitled to choose an insurance plan. That is Obamacare's job.

When Obama was at George Mason University in Virginia right before the 2012 election, he said, "Let me tell you something, Virginia. I don't think your boss should control the care you get. I don't think insurance companies should… I definitely don't think politicians on Capitol Hill should… I think there's one person who gets to make decisions about your health care—that's you."[65] This came from the person who instituted a massive new regulatory health care law that not only coerces everyone to take part but dictates everything we must take part in. The new welfare age means free stuff paid for by others, and the government decides what the "stuff" will be; it decides for "you."

Alms to the State

Markets can work out competing differences peacefully, because there is no coercion involved. But when the state creates virtual monopolies through regulatory regimes, it also gets to decide what is moral and necessary and compels everyone to act accordingly. Most of us who aren't Catholic, it's fair to say, are not interested in having the Catholic Church dictate the moral contours of our lives, but surely we should be equally uninterested in having the Obama administration do so. The dogmatism of the left is no less—in fact is manifestly more—intrusive than the actions of the Catholic Church. When was the last time, after all, that the Catholic Church banned you from drinking a large soda as Mayor Bloomberg did in New York, or forbade you from choosing the light bulb of your choice as the federal government did, or coerced you to drop money into the collection plate on a Sunday, unlike the IRS that demands it de facto every day of the week?

Let's pause for a moment and introduce the great Jewish philosopher Mosheh ben Maimon, better known to the world as Maimonides. Perhaps the most distinguished medieval Jewish philosopher, Maimonides was also a biblical scholar and one of the great physicians of the Middle Ages. In one of many useful treatises, Maimonides laid out the eight levels of charity available to men.[66] The two least moral brands of charity, he noted, were when a person offers up assistance inadequately but gives it with a smile; and worse, when a person gives charity unwillingly, because then it really isn't charity at all.

At the top of Maimonides' list, as the best form of charity, was something Milton Friedman and Friedrich Hayek would have approved: "There is no greater giving than to support a fellow Jew by endowing him with a gift or loan, or entering into a partnership with him, or finding employment for him, in order to strengthen his hand until he need no longer be dependent upon others."

The Bible's view of charity (not to mention a Jewish philosopher's take on the issue) might seem irrelevant to the policy of a secular state, but as a shared moral understanding about charity, and healthy societies can only exist with certain shared moral understandings, it makes a lot of sense. Economically speaking, there used to be little argument about the most effective way of giving: it was to help the poor and unfortunate become as self-sufficient as possible, to encourage work and personal responsibility. At the very least it was to encourage, through a free economy, the creation of more wealth, which in turn would create more jobs (and make available more money for charity).

Liberals, however, purposefully conflate coerced giving with charity.

Some Democrats have gone so far as to make the case that Jesus would vote for Democrats because that party's budget better reflects the moral and charitable understanding of a good Christian. My favorite such essay came from a Harvard professor named, (in)appropriately enough, Erika Christakis, writing in *Time* magazine:[67]

> Americans often tell pollsters they yearn for a return to the Christian principles on which the U.S. was founded. If so, they should take a closer look at the Mitt Romney–Paul Ryan ticket. Jesus' teachings regarding wealth are nowhere to be found in Ryan's budget proposal.
>
> As near as we can tell, Jesus would advocate a tax rate somewhere between 50% (in the vein of "If you have two coats, give one to the man who has none") and 100% (if you want to get into heaven, be poor). Mostly, he suggested giving all your money up for the benefit of others. And Jesus made no distinction between the deserving and undeserving poor; his love and generosity applied to all.

As near as we can tell, Jesus did not advocate for tax policy; and his calls, after all, were for individuals to make these sacrifices of their own free will. But since we can all play the game of "what would Jesus do?," I think it's fair to assume that he'd flatten income taxes and lower capital gains taxes because the most moral policies are those that create more jobs and create more wealth, which genuinely benefit the poor... and because, surely, as in the parable of the talents, he was in favor of investments that earned big dividends. It's funny though that liberals rail against the idea of mixing God and politics...except when they do it. When conservatives do it—pardon the expression—all hell breaks loose.

During the 2012 campaign, vice presidential candidate Paul Ryan told the Christian Broadcasting Network about how his Catholic faith informed his conservative political beliefs, in part through the Catholic social and political principle of "subsidiarity," which, as he explained it, is a bit like federalism, in that the Church believes in the necessity of subsidiary institutions like the Church and the family and voluntary organizations that stand as a buffer between the individual and the state. "Through our civic organizations, through our churches, through our charities," he said, "through all of our different groups where we interact with people as a community, that's how we advance the common good, by not having Big Government crowd out civic society, but by having enough space in our communities so that we can interact with each other, and take care of people who are down and out in our communities."[68]

Democrats were simply appalled, because they believe they have a lock on morality, and that we measure it by how much we empower and enrich the state to do moral—or allegedly moral—things for us. Where Catholics look to priests, Protestants to pastors, and Jews to rabbis, secular liberals look to bureaucrats with the coercive power of the state; and government-imposed "morality" crowds out morality in communities. But who really cares about the poor, do you think? There are numerous studies that have found that conservatives give more to charity. A *Chronicle of Philanthropy* poll recently found that citizens in red states are more prone to offer charitable donations than those in blue states. The eight states where residents gave the highest share of their income were Mormon Utah (number one), deeply conservative Idaho, and the Bible Belt "religious right" states of Mississippi, Alabama, Tennessee, South Carolina, Arkansas, and Georgia. The average citizen of Utah gives 10.6 percent of his income to charity. The least generous states were Wisconsin, Connecticut, Rhode Island, Massachusetts, Vermont, Maine, and (last) New Hampshire (where the average resident gave 2.5 percent of his income).[69]

My own view, and the conservative view, is that charity is a private matter. Our charity is not measured by government budgets. Budgets should be actuarial documents—namely, balanced. And though it might feel counterintuitive to some, we should have the moral sense to recognize that capitalism (which introduced fossil fuels, factories, cities, cars—all the things that dismay the average progressive) has done more to lift people from poverty than all government programs combined. Morality—in every sense, from means like personal responsibility to ends like helping the poor—thrives when government is limited. If you don't believe me, here's what Catholic intellectual Robert P. George of Princeton University said about the proper role of government:[70]

> What are the obligations and purposes of law and government?
>
> (1) To protect (a) public health, (b) safety, and (c) morals, and (2) to advance the general welfare—including, preeminently, protecting people's fundamental rights and basic liberties.

Wouldn't this require the granting of vast and sweeping powers to public authority?

No; the general welfare—the common good—requires that government be limited.

You distinguish between government's primary and subsidiary roles. What are the government's primary responsibilities?

Government's responsibility is primary when the questions involve (1) defending the nation from attack and subversion, (2) protecting people from physical assaults and various other forms of depredation, and (3) maintaining public order.

That the common good requires limited government is not a radical idea; it's an idea of the Founding Fathers; one could even see it as a biblical idea (many American colonists did). Not everyone agrees, of course. "I am afraid that Chairman Ryan's budget reflects the values of his favorite philosopher Ayn Rand rather than the gospel of Jesus Christ," wrote Thomas J. Reese, a leftist Jesuit. "Survival of the fittest may be okay for Social Darwinists but not for followers of the gospel of compassion and love."[71] Likewise, *Washington Post* columnist E. J. Dionne, a Catholic Democrat, believes an "unfettered lightly taxed market economy"[72] is a radical idea. (What would the Founders have thought of that?) His fellow scribbler at the *Washington Post*, Greg Sargent, agreed that the Romney/Ryan budget was "a radical vision when it comes to the proper distribution of wealth,"[73] as if there is a "proper" way to distribute wealth other than by earning it in a job or by investing it in the market—is that a radical idea?

Speaking at Georgetown University, Ryan contended that there could be a "difference of opinion between faithful Catholics on this issue"—which was a nice change of pace from the moralistic scorn of the left. But he also pointed out the fact that massive government spending had done little to help the poor: we now have the highest poverty rate in a generation. "In this war on poverty, poverty is winning," he said. There must be a better way.[74] It should not be radical to say that charitable giving to help those who can't help themselves or who need a temporary helping hand is one thing; coercive government that takes from some to make dependents of others is something else entirely. It should be obvious; but to leftists, it's not. Morality and coercion are not the same thing—in fact, they are opposites—and making the poor and the middle class reliant on the government is not morality; it is immoral dependency.

The 47 Percent (and Why They're Never Going Away)

So once you've embedded a dependency culture into the moral fabric of the nation, what happens to our democracy? What happens to our institutions? What happens when politicians can win elections by promising a welfare state rather than a meritocracy?

No doubt many of you remember that during the 2012 presidential campaign, Republican nominee Mitt Romney was clandestinely recorded uttering a conclusion about the electorate that was factually and ideologically confused, if not entirely inaccurate. In a meeting with donors, Romney essentially wrote off 47 percent of Americans. He claimed this 47 percent "believe that they are victims," that "government has a responsibility to care for them," and they will never "take personal responsibility and care for their lives."[75]

Romney, it seems, was basing his "47 percent" calculation on the number of Americans who don't pay any federal income tax. This is wrongheaded in a number of ways. To begin with, many voters who don't pay income taxes are either elderly or young, or haven't earned enough to pay federal income taxes, or are middle class families with children who are barely under the income barrier. Nor is the 47 percent static. Many Americans fluctuate from being payers to being non-payers and back again. Politically speaking, though, Romney's calculus was a disaster. Asserting that half the country is made up of moochers isn't exactly a cheery, forward-looking message that we're looking for from our leaders (even if it were true). Romney tried to avoid talking about "the 47 percent" for the remainder of the campaign. Conversely, Obama grabbed hold of the incident and plugged it into his larger narrative about the Republican challenger: Romney was a plutocrat who misunderstood the average American (probably true).

Alas, after the election Romney went back to the same theme. The *Los Angeles Times* reported that the defeated candidate told donors during a conference call that the Obama campaign won because it was "focused on giving targeted groups a big gift" and was "very generous" to ethnic minorities and young voters.[76]

Romney was on to something, even if he put it in a politically maladroit way. Florida Senator Marco Rubio, criticizing Romney's remarks, put it differently, and showed himself a better politician, saying he didn't "believe that we have millions and millions of people in this country that don't want to work… I think we have millions of people in this country that are out of work and are dependent on the government because they can't find a job."[77] Fair enough, although, to be honest, he downplayed the way that government is a pusher of dependency and how easily people can be hooked into a lifestyle that hurts them.

As you can imagine, other potential 2016 Republican candidates—including New Jersey governor Chris Christie, former Speaker

of the House Newt Gingrich, and Wisconsin governor Scott Walker—
revved up their indignation over Romney's post-election comments.
Speaking to reporters at an annual meeting of Republican governors,
Louisiana governor Bobby Jindal said the GOP could no longer afford
to be as divisive as Romney had been. "I think that's absolutely wrong.
We have got to stop dividing the American voters," he went on. "We
need to go after 100 percent of the votes, not 53 percent. We need to
go after every single vote.... So I absolutely reject that notion, that
description. I think it's absolutely wrong. I don't think that represents
where we are as a party and where we're going as a party. That has
got to be one of the most fundamental takeaways from this election."[78]

Of course, a major political party has to chase every single vote.
Of course, a president represents every single American citizen, not
just the ones that are already prone to vote for him. But if handouts
were irrelevant to voters, politicians wouldn't promise them; they
wouldn't offer to bail out student loans or mortgages or businesses;
they wouldn't hand out ethanol subsidies or corporate tax breaks or
union bailouts; and they certainly wouldn't, as Obama did, base an
entire presidential term and campaign on the morality of redistributing wealth. Republicans need to appeal for every vote and make
persuasive arguments for their policy prescriptions, but it would be
foolish not to see that the more people are induced into dependency,
the harder it will be to promote the ideals of limited government.
There was a lot of talk about racial demographics dooming the
Republican Party, but the dependency demographics are just as dire.

Republicans actually did try to make the argument against dependency during the 2012 campaign. Presidential candidate Rick Santo-
rum said that President Obama was getting America hooked on "the
narcotic of dependency." Candidate Romney warned that government

programs "foster passivity and sloth." *New York Times* columnist Paul Krugman criticized Paul Ryan for admiring Ayn Rand's novel *Atlas Shrugged*, in which, a helpful Krugman explained, "heroic capitalists struggle against the 'moochers' trying to steal their totally deserved wealth, a struggle the heroes win by withdrawing their productive effort and giving interminable speeches."[79] It was no secret that Republicans stood against the ever-expanding welfare state that Obama favors. But never had Americans had a bigger stake in that welfare state.

In 2007, the Campbell Public Affairs Institute's Maxwell Poll sifted through the data regarding welfare use and politics. Eighty-one percent of voters who received government-subsidized housing voted for Democrats, as did 80 percent of food stamp recipients, 79 percent of those receiving unemployment compensation, 78 percent of those on welfare, 75 percent of those on disability benefits, and 74 percent of those who use Medicaid.[80] These aren't the only government dependents; in 2012, unionized government workers preferred Obama over Romney by 59 percent to 34 percent. When government grows—and it does nothing but—it expands its base of supporters; dependency is a winning game for the Democrats. So let's not pretend it's got nothing to do with politics.

Then there are taxes. One of the most significant reasons we have a growing dependency state is our tax structure. It was Harry Hopkins, one of Franklin Roosevelt's most calculating advisors, who laid out the winning formula for elections: "We will spend and spend, and tax and tax, and elect and elect." These days, the entire economic policy of the Democratic Party relies on taking from one person and giving it to another. For Democrats, detesting the rich is an enormously rewarding pastime, and they've managed to convince the majority of us that the wealthy should pay even more in income taxes (the top 10 percent of earners already carry more than 70 percent of the load of federal income taxes).

But however popular it is, there are at least two reasons why robbing the rich to pay for government handouts for the rest of us is a path to doom.

First, we are feeding a self-perpetuating system that disconnects people from the cost of government. No doubt, a skewed tax structure allows Obama to spread the wealth around to those who deserve it—clean energy outfits, teachers' unions, policy czars, unemployed Black Panthers, etc.—but it also creates a growing number of voters with little stake in limiting government, even as it bankrupts the country. These voters trust that someone else—the wealthy—will always foot the bill; big government politicians have given them no reason to think otherwise. In 2011, it was estimated that 45 percent of U.S. households paid not a single dollar in federal income tax.[81] As the *Fiscal Times* reported, "For the first time since the Great Depression, households are receiving more income from the government than they are paying the government in taxes."[82] In New York City, only 1.2 percent of the taxpayers pay 50 percent of the income taxes—while 50 percent of households pay no income tax at all.[83] Obama likes to go on endlessly about how we need to "sacrifice" for the common good. But for increasing numbers of Americans, there is no sacrifice. Government is simply the great provider, and they are the recipients—at least until everything comes crashing down. If, as the enlightened voices on the left contend, the American people deeply love their federal services, their dependency programs, their regulations, their industrious public education department, why shouldn't *everyone* pay more to ensure their survival?

Second, if we don't broaden the tax base, we'll continue to see less revenue and increased economic stagnation. It's true that lower tax rates free up capital, which in turn creates jobs, which in turn increases revenues to the government—a win, win, win—but beyond the pragmatic argument is the moral one. As a simple matter of, yes, fairness, everyone, even the rich—even the super-filthy rich—deserves to be treated equally by their government. Just as we all, in America, stand equal in the sight of the law, so should we stand equal before the taxman. The fairest tax rate is a flat tax rate. It is also best for the common good. As Joseph Thorndike, a historian with the Tax History Project, explained to *USA Today*, a broadening of the tax base would be healthy for the nation. "If you ask people to pay something then they have an ownership stake in it," Thorndike said. "The narrow, soak-the-rich approach is real short-sighted politics."[84]

Republicans could win an award for shortsightedness, because they were the ones who worked so assiduously to get people (not the rich, but the lower middle class) off the tax rolls. Democrats have been shortsighted too but in a different way. Somehow Democrats refuse to see that when they "soak the rich," the rich respond by investing less, opening fewer businesses, hiring fewer people, and spending less money. So soaking the rich really means soaking everybody else too.

There's another aspect of dependency politics that's too often neglected, and that's the crony capitalism practiced by the Obama administration. It has been rather surreal to watch so many Democrats celebrate the president's courageous use of taxpayer money to bail out companies and allow them to avoid bankruptcy. This is now called "economic patriotism," and it is one area of dependency that can be abruptly ended if a truly fiscal conservative ever sees the inside of the White House again.

Remember when Obama said, "I don't want to run auto companies, and I don't want to run banks"?[85] Well, he changed his mind in a big way. Obama, speaking in the depressed city of Pueblo, Colorado, heaped praise upon himself for his uncanny ability to use other people's money to nationalize unproductive companies: "I said, I believe in American workers, I believe in this American industry, and now the American auto industry has come roaring back. Now I want to do the same thing with manufacturing jobs, not just in the auto industry, but in every industry."[86]

Every industry!

When Obama sold the taxpayers' interest in Chrysler a little more than a year ago, we were out $1.3 billion. Taxpayers are still "invested" with 25 percent of General Motors' stocks, which, if sold today, could mean another $16 to $20 billion in losses. Taxpayers would only break even on GM if the price of a share was $53 (as of this writing it's less than half that). But, of course, that's not the worst part of the bailout. It's the moral hazard—the cronyism. Rather than allowing companies to shed the burden of labor contracts and their failing business models, the Obama administration has been busy playing politics. It administered its own "bankruptcy," punishing stakeholders and certain workers and rewarding unions and other cronies—and, let's not forget, ignoring the rule of law. Every time other unproductive manufacturers run into trouble, can they expect Washington to bail them out? Or maybe the president means he will preemptively save them?

Obama cronyism has been, if anything, even more blatant in so-called "Green Energy"—because, while he talks about jobs and economic growth, it has only to do with moralism not economics. Though the United States government wastes tens of billions of dollars on an array of these unproductive companies, Solyndra was the most egregious example of recent corporate welfare, filing for bankruptcy and costing taxpayers $535 million in loan guarantees.

It Ends Badly

If you believe government can transform you into a more moral, productive, or successful person, you deserve what's coming to you. The problem is that we're all about to get what's coming to us. America was once a place where citizens who found themselves in unfortunate circumstances had to figure out a way to survive without a government safety net, which meant either using their own devices or accepting help from independent charitable institutions, often connected to churches. Now, the majority Democratic Party is entirely based on the idea that the moral imperative of the age is to make more and more people dependent on government.

America used to be a land of many vibrant churches. Tocqueville noted them as one of the strengths of our society. There are still plenty of churches, but we are now all supposed to submit to the Church of Obama, or of the State; it determines our morality for us and coerces us to finance its decisions.

Some day, perhaps soon, it all will come crashing down. The welfare state creates unsustainable debt. It also rearranges government spending priorities in ways that can be suicidal. As Robert Samuelson, the superb columnist for the *Washington Post*, points out, "President Obama's budget assumes that defense spending, as a share of the economy, falls 39 percent from 2011 to 2022. The Army is to drop by 80,000 soldiers, the Marines, 20,000. Domestic 'discretionary' spending is cut even more, 45 percent. Research, education, transportation, law enforcement and other programs face pressures."[87] Whatever you make of United States foreign policy, defense should be the primary function of government. And no one really thinks Obama intends to balance the budget by drastic cuts in discretionary spending, so government is going to go bust before it gets out of the red.

Big government makes us poorer; it does so by making us less moral. It undermines our work ethic; it rewards irresponsibility (through everything from mortgage bailouts to subsidized contraception); it promotes envy and greed; it creates enemy classes or groups (like the wealthy) and encourages us all to demonize them and take from them. As we learned from an instructional video at the Democratic National Convention, "We do believe you can use government in a good way. Government is the only thing we all belong to."

The Founding Fathers didn't believe that we "belonged to" government. If we belonged to anyone beyond ourselves it was to God. Government belonged to the people and was not supposed to trample on their life, liberty, or pursuit of happiness.

But things have changed. Government knows best. Though with $16 trillion in debt—$100 trillion if you factor in unfunded liabilities[88]—maybe not. "Government," of course, won't pay that, and neither can "the wealthy"; we will.

CHAPTER THREE

PARTY LIKE THERE'S NO TOMORROW

"Today, I am pledging to cut the deficit we inherited in half by the end of my first term in office. This will not be easy. It will require us to make difficult decisions and face challenges we have long neglected. But I refuse to leave our children with a debt that they cannot repay—and that means taking responsibility right now, in this Administration, for getting our spending under control."
—BARACK OBAMA, FISCAL RESPONSIBILITY SUMMIT, FEBRUARY 23, 2009

"Who goeth a borrowing goeth a sorrowing."
—THOMAS TUSSER

"If you owe the bank a hundred thousand dollars, the bank owns you. If you owe the bank a hundred million dollars, you own the bank."
—AMERICAN PROVERB
(FROM DAVID GRAEBER'S *DEBT: THE FIRST 5,000 YEARS*)

Math will get you every time

"Every election is a sort of advance auction sale of stolen goods," wrote one of the great twentieth century skeptics, H. L. Mencken. Well, President Barack Obama did Mencken one better and auctioned off what he was going to steal from generations yet to be born.

Forward, indeed.

There are a lot of ways to look at the national debt, and every angle promises to be more depressing than the previous one. That's not to say Americans don't care about debt. We certainly think we do. Before the 2012 elections, Gallup asked Americans what worried them most about the economy. First was jobs, second was debt.[1] Nearly every recent poll shows that people are anxious about deficit spending—or at least they like to tell pollsters that they're worried. In turn, most politicians return the favor by *pretending* to care about deficit spending, though they keep blowing through dollars, at ever more rapid rates, in the name of "stimulus" or "green energy" or whatever "investment" happens to be fashionable that day. As reporter Terrence P. Jeffrey noted, "in the less-than-three-years Obama has been in office," at the end of September 2011, "the federal debt has increased by $4.212 trillion—more than the total national debt of about $4.1672 trillion accumulated by all 41 U.S. presidents from George Washington through George H. W. Bush combined."[2]

The numbers are so huge, and we've grown so used to them, that the national debt can seem a distant, abstract threat—like a giant comet hitting the earth far off in the future. Still, amassing enormous debt certainly didn't hurt Obama's reelection campaign; and Democratic politicians don't seem afraid of employing increased debt as policy. To them the deficit is more of an outward symbol of how charitable public servants can be with your money. Inevitably, though, deficit spending leads to a day of reckoning—a day every adult used to experience—when the bills have to be paid. If America's liberal politicians ignore that fact, America's enemies haven't. Iranian President

Mahmoud Ahmadinejad has made a habit of portending American ruin. Most of his predictions, needless to say, are absolutely bonkers. But the Islamic revolutionary did offer a rather uncomfortable query near the end of 2012 that most American politicians refuse to ask themselves: "How long," he said during a press conference, "can a government with a $16 trillion foreign debt remain a world power?"[3]

The answer could be, "Not so very long at all." Our collapse won't happen overnight. We have amassed too many advantages for an abrupt demise. Our economic, cultural, and political capital might be rapidly dwindling, but it still exists, and even with a stagnant American economic dystopia on the horizon, there will still be, we can hope, enough of the old country's positives attributes left to keep it far preferable to life under the imams in Iran. But what we now know as America—a world power brimming with the type of prosperity and opportunity we're used to—will be over. Soon enough we will have to recalibrate what prosperity means. Someday we will have to answer Ahmadinejad's question. How long can we carry $16 trillion of debt and remain a world power? Actually, by the time we're compelled to act on the national debt, it likely won't be $16 trillion; we'll be talking about $20 or $30 or $40 trillion, because when it comes to deficit spending, there's no end in sight.

Sure, our country has been in debt before, but it was manageable, and with healthy economic growth and mildly conscientious budgeting, we beat it. More recently, though, we have come to accept massive and growing debt as a normal state of being—so much so that we reelected a president who treats deficit spending as if it were the most effective way to restore America's economic power rather than the most effective way to destroy it. But, in the end, even political victories can't outrun the overwhelming force of arithmetic. Soon enough, that debt will overtake our institutions and the electorate will be faced with an ugly choice: austerity or ruin. Inevitably, we will then have to recalibrate our definitions of prosperity and freedom.

Even before D-Day arrives—today even—debilitating debt inhibits American economic dynamism; our economy can't expand fast enough to overpower such an enormous deficit. How big a crisis is it? Navy Admiral Mike Mullen, chairman of the Joint Chiefs of Staff, speaking to a group of business leaders, warned that "the single, biggest threat to our national security is our debt" and that "we have every responsibility to help eliminate that threat."[4] Debt, in other words, is a bigger threat to our future than global terrorism, or out-of-control bankers, or obesity, or even climate change, if you can imagine that. Speaking to the Business Executives for National Security, Admiral Mullen went on to say: "All of you have dealt with downturns in the business cycle. Many of you have turned around troubled corporations, or restructured firms. Our challenges will not precisely be yours, but I'll bet we can take a lesson or two from what you've seen."

If only. In the last presidential election, the American people had a choice between a successful businessman and the biggest deficit spender in American history, and they plumped for the spender.

So maybe it has a lot to do with us? In a democracy, government reflects the sensibilities of its people, and many of its people have bad habits. Study after study shows us that Americans themselves are taking on more debt than they can handle—so it's not surprising, I guess, that we do the same collectively. One of the core reasons for the recession (and we tend to forget this part) wasn't only that Wall Street devils were profiting from bundled toxic subprime mortgage stocks, but that throngs of citizens were shacking up in houses they couldn't really afford, making those risky stocks a possibility. Democrats always blame the drug pusher and never the user.

According to a study led by Sherman Hanna, professor of consumer sciences at Ohio State University, "gross personal financial mismanagement," going beyond mortgage and credit card markets, is happening in all strata of America society. The study found that default or bankruptcy becomes likely after household debt reaches 40 percent of income.[5] The percentage of Americans exceeding the 40 percent threshold jumped from 17 percent in 1992 to 27 percent in 2008. Since the recession, the median net worth of American families has fallen by nearly 40 percent, from $126,400 in 2007 to $77,300 in 2010,[6] and this has forced us to be a bit more responsible in our spending—and borrowing. Even so, and even with government bailouts of mortgages, Americans still hold more than $1 trillion of personal delinquent debt. Nearly $800 billion is overdue by more than 90 days. Perhaps the most interesting fact about the Ohio State University study was that those who described themselves as "most optimistic about the future" were also the most likely to own unmanageable debt. "People who piled on debt may have been too optimistic about their economic future," explained Hanna, "but you can't blame that on a lack of education. People with college educations may have thought they were immune to any economic problems." Highly educated Americans were—and are—more likely to assume unmanageable liabilities. I suppose if you're a highly educated American with a sense of entitlement and the ability to rack up debt, you can afford to have a rosy view of the future—just like the Obama administration.

So it's probably not surprising that our politicians are as disconnected from the fiscal reality of debt as are many of their constituents. Both the voters and the politicians appear to think that if it comes right down to it, they'll either be able to stick "the wealthy" with the bill, or default with impunity. Neither is an even remotely realistic scenario. America has about 3 million millionaires. Even if we taxed them a million dollars a piece, and devoted all that money exclusively to paying off the debt, we'd still be short by 13 trillion dollars on the debt, and somehow have to come up with another 4 trillion dollars to meet the federal budget. Defaulting on our debts essentially means welcoming an economic contraction so severe that you might as well call it a second great depression. Not much hope in that, but certainly a lot of change.

Devilish Debt

Debt does have its uses—aside from getting Democrats elected. In reality, we wouldn't want a world *completely* free of debt. Thomas Jefferson's rule that you should "never spend your money before you have it,"[7] isn't exactly right (and he didn't exactly follow it). Prudence, thrift, and no-nonsense frugality were once embedded in our national identity, but there's really nothing inherently wrong with borrowing money—not in our personal lives or in broader economic policy—within limits. Taking on a mortgage, after all, used to be a sign of responsibility. It showed that one was up to the task of becoming a homeowner and making regular payments. When government is healthy and behaving rationally, there are beneficial reasons to borrow as well. For instance, debt enables government to equalize expenditures over long periods of time so that it can engage in large-scale infrastructure projects that can abet future economic growth. In our personal lives, most of us carry some level of debt and it makes our lives immeasurably more comfortable and rewarding. If we had to immediately pay the entire cost of a car, or a home, or a four-year college education, many of us simply could not afford these items, at least not without deferring them for a very long time.

Borrowing in this sense actually helps our economy function and grow.

The trouble with the modern federal government in general and the Obama administration in particular is that it inverts the morality of responsible borrowing—namely, that one never takes on more debt than one can expect to pay back over a reasonable time, and that one never borrows frivolously. While Americans have traditionally believed that the morality of borrowing was defined by a responsible making of payments, the federal government and the Obama administration have made a virtue of deficit spending, acting as if federal and state government workers—principal beneficiaries of "stimulus" spending—indebted college students, growing caseloads of welfare recipients, participants in entitlement programs, and bankrupt "green" energy companies are engines of American economic growth. The fact is, they are not. And all of us, but especially the young, are going to pay a terrible price when the bill comes due.

Blessed Are the Young for They Shall Inherit the National Debt[8]

On January 20, 2009, the day President Barack Obama was inaugurated and saved the nation from the clutches of runaway capitalism, the national debt was $10,626,877,048,913.08; Obama, acting more irresponsibly than any Wall Street villain, increased that by around $6,000,000,000,000.[9] If Barack Obama paid the debt back a dollar a second it would only take him 126,750 presidential terms to "finish the job" and put us back on solid fiscal ground. Assuming the debt didn't grow in the meantime.

The very fact that the debt is so large also makes it perversely imaginary. So let's start with some smaller numbers. Right now, the United States spends more than $220 billion just paying the interest on the national debt,[10] which is around the same we spend annually on expenditures on Medicaid. And it gets worse. According to the Congressional Budget Office and the Office of Budget Management, within a decade federal spending on the interest on America's debt will exceed the total spending of the defense budget by more than a $125 billion.[11]

In 2012, the United States Congress asked for a $3.729 trillion budget and it enacted a $3.796 trillion budget—because no budget is ever large enough, obviously.[12] In 2012, the federal budget deficit topped $1 trillion for the fourth straight year—every year of the Obama presidency. To put that recklessness in deeper perspective think about this: the Treasury Department calculated that the 2012 budget year amassed $1.1 trillion in debt, despite the fact that tax revenue had *risen* by 6.4 percent from the year before and despite the fact that, believe it or not, the rate of government spending had actually *fallen* by 1.7 percent—mostly because Congress couldn't pull together a budget and because U.S. military involvement in Iraq was winding down.[13]

Right now, the U.S. debt the public holds, which does not include money owed to Social Security and other government trust funds, tops 60 percent of the entire economy of the United States as measured by gross domestic product. In other words, if the federal government were a household it would be well beyond the 40 percent debt threshold and well on the way to default, bankruptcy, and ruin. And sure enough, we are. By 2022, less than ten years away, the debt is projected to reach 100 percent of GDP. By 2035, it's on track to reach 200 percent. By comparison, between 1960 and 2000 the public held, on average, debt that amounted to 37 percent of GDP, according to information from the debt reduction task force.[14] In a March

2012 report from the General Accounting Office we are warned that between 2020 and 2030, the amount of spending on entitlements and interest could outpace all federal revenues.[15]

All right, that all sounds chilling, but surely we're better off than Europe? Well, actually, no. The U.S. Treasury Department federal budget deficit for the *month* of October 2012 was $120 billion.[16] That's more than the 2011 *annual* deficits of Greece ($9 billion), Spain ($29 billion), and Italy ($87 billion) *combined*. In one month, the United States matched the entire annual deficit spending of three European nations on the brink of bankruptcy and social upheaval. Only Japan, Britain, France, and Mexico produced *annual* 2011 deficits that surpassed a single *month* of our own.[17]

No doubt you're thinking: hey, we're a huge country, so obviously Americans are going to produce larger deficits—even in one month— than most nations will generate in a year. One could easily argue the opposite, actually. America *is* a far wealthier nation, so it shouldn't have to produce large annual deficits; and shouldn't we be less inclined to rack up huge debt than socialist-leaning Euro states that have only a fraction of our own economic output? It's not like we measure up well against Europe on a per capita basis either. As Republican Senator Jeff Sessions, ranking member on the Senate Budget Committee, pointed out recently, America's per capita government debt is worse than that of Greece, Ireland, Italy, France, Portugal, and Spain.[18]

"He that dies pays all his debts," wrote William Shakespeare. Well, not exactly. Rather than measuring what we—you and I—owe on the national credit card, let's talk about all those unfortunate little people in our lives. What will kids inherit from our abysmal legacy of debt? Liberals, after all, are incessantly warning us about the need to leave a better world behind for the children. Perhaps the most helpful analysis on this front was offered by the folks at CNS News Service who measured what Americans under the age of 18 would be required to pay off if we asked them to pony up for the entirety of the federal government's debt in equal shares. Each young American would already be presented with a bill of about $220,000.[19] That's more than the median price of a house; more than four years of college education—and in fact if you factor in the debt they'll take on as college students with government loans, they're going to be really in the hole. Under Obama, student debt has jumped 74 percent to about a trillion dollars. If you think credit card debt is a problem, you'll be glad to know that student debt, measured in terms of delinquent payments, is worse and that more than 9 percent of students default on their debts within two years of trying to repay them. That's bad news for them—or really it's bad news for everybody, because as the think tank AEI pointed out, if students go the way of bad mortgages with "government 'forgiveness' of student loan debt, it will simply be one more example of fiscal subsidies for a narrow demographic."[20] In other words, robbing Tyler to pay Madison. Oh, and it will also add another trillion or so in debt—and guess who'll eventually have to pay that?

So debt is scary, or it should be, but it's also complicated.

For one thing, all debt is not created equal. Our overall debt includes federally amassed debt plus intergovernmental borrowing, money that the U.S. government has loaned itself from one part of the budget to another, like transfers to Social Security. Some cite this fact to diminish the president's part in propagating the problem. Good luck with that. Since Obama took office, publicly held debt has increased from about $6 trillion to about $11 trillion—nearly 80 percent. Similarly, some pundits like to belittle the consequences of any obligations we have to ourselves, because, they argue, tapping your own funds isn't necessarily as terrible as borrowing from, say, the Chinese or the Saudis. One: the opposite is true. Though the Chinese and Saudis will still dislike us, and we them, when they invest in the United States their future becomes tethered to ours and they have a vested interest in making sure that we can pay them back. Two: if you believe lending yourself money is a healthy way to run a budget, try writing yourself an I.O.U. and cashing it at your local bank.

But Democrats—and most of the media—continue to assert that Social Security does not contribute to federal deficits and the national debt, because this is money we owe ourselves. White House press secretary Jay Carney, for example, has said categorically, "We should address the drivers of the deficit, and Social Security is not currently a driver of the deficit—that's an economic fact." Senator Dick Durbin of Illinois, during the debate over the fiscal cliff at the end of 2012, said, "Social Security does not add one penny to our debt, not a penny."

How could one of the largest budget items not add to the debt? Some fancy juggling of numbers. Even so, here are the facts: In 2011, Social Security added $48 billion to the deficit. In 2012, Social Security added around $50 billion to the deficit. In 2015, the Congressional Budget Office says Social Security will add $86.6 billion to the deficit. We live longer, have fewer children, and promise more. How could Social Security not be a problem moving forward? If things stay the way they are, Social Security carries around $22 *trillion* in unfunded liabilities. Our government is making promises our revenues can't cash.

All the estimates and numbers above, however scary they sound, still fail to instill this problem with the justice it deserves. First of all, the calculations typically project present-day Obama budgets outward. Unless a serious epidemic of rational thinking sweeps over the administration, those numbers will undoubtedly swell over the next few years. Then there is the issue of future costs. Costs we can't measure. Costs we probably don't want to measure.

Though the bureaucratic class in Washington will never admit it, we have no way to forecast debt with any certainty because we have no way to forecast revenue or government expenditure with any certainty, though it seems fair to assume that the Entitlement State will keep growing and cost more than government bookkeepers estimate. As Michael Tanner and Chris Edwards of the libertarian Cato Institute have pointed out,[21] government accountants have a penchant for dramatically miscalculating—that is, considerably underestimating—the cost of state-run programs.

That's not surprising, but the degree of the miscalculations might even shock a cynic. For example, Part A of Medicare, launched in 1965, was projected to cost $9 billion by 1990. It ended up costing $67 billion. Medicaid's hospital subsidy, added in 1987, was estimated to cost taxpayers $100 million a year. Only five years later, it was costing *$11 billion* a year. Medicare's home care benefit, added in 1988, was projected to cost $4 billion in 1993, but ended up costing $10 billion. Romneycare, the Massachusetts forerunner to Obamacare, was enacted in 2006, with a price tag of $725 million a year; its cost is now over $1 billion.[22] And estimated costs for Obamacare itself are rapidly escalating, even though the bulk of the program hasn't even been instituted yet.[23]

The numbers are mind-boggling—current estimates are in the range of $1,856 billion from 2012 to 2022—but the fact is Obamacare has the potential to generate almost incalculable future liabilities. Since Obamacare blankets the entire health care industry, it leaves the door wide open for politicians to expand costly programs in the future, just as Medicare has been expanded, but even more so. Chuck

Blahous, a widely respected and experienced researcher and analyst—appointed by President Obama as a trustee of the Social Security and Medicare programs—released a peer-reviewed study that found the Affordable Care Act (Obamacare) is "expected to add at least $340 billion and as much as $530 billion to federal deficits while increasing federal spending by more than $1.15 trillion…and by increasing amounts thereafter."[24] Medicare and Social Security are already "on unsustainable paths" and will be insolvent within a few decades—according to the annual report of the funds' trustees.[25] Social Security is projected to run a $937 billion deficit from 2013 through 2022.[26] And it's hard to imagine how Obamacare does anything more than give us yet another gigantic and ultimately untenable government program to explode our national debt.

Consequences Schmonsequences

The most damning aspect of this looming crisis is that the Democratic Party has transformed into an organization that isn't just ignoring the problem, but is in many ways actively pro-debt. Obama once lambasted George W. Bush for adding a measly $4 trillion to the national debt over his eight years in office. He called it "irresponsible" and "unpatriotic."[27] But once he was given the keys, he made George W. Bush look like a piker, increasing the debt 50 percent, or $6 trillion, in less than four years.[28] He's on a track to triple Bush's increase over eight years. Imagine how much more he would have spent if those obstructionist Republicans in Congress hadn't been in his way. Instead of "fixing" the debt crisis, the Obama administration took America's already dismal debt numbers and showed the country how it was done.

Though occasionally referring to the debt with alarmed tones, the president has taken no ownership of the crisis. When asked about the debt in an interview that aired on September 12, 2012, on CBS's *60 Minutes*, the president blamed "90 percent" of the deficit "as a consequence of two wars that weren't paid for, as a consequence of tax cuts that weren't paid for, a prescription drug plan that was not paid for, and then the worst economic crisis since the Great Depression." His "emergency actions," he said, are responsible "for about 10 percent of this increase in the deficit."[29]

He's having fun with math, creatively conflating competing numbers. He was also having some fun with history, as Democrats had fought for a more expensive prescription drug program and had voted for "unpaid" wars themselves. But the most damning fact is that Obama has never supported any genuine reform that would ease the nation's debt burden. He has shown no interest in reducing the size of government. Quite the opposite. In fact, nearly every signature achievement of the Obama administration costs more than a mid-sized country's annual GDP, and the administration has not come close to covering these costs. Using Treasury Department data, conservative scholar Jeffrey H. Anderson discovered that government spending outpaced tax revenues by a trillion dollars, or to put it a different way, the Obama administration spent 44 percent more than it had coming in. This was actually an improvement from fiscal year 2011 (56 percent) and fiscal year 2010 (60 percent).[30] So, progress.

But here's the stunning fact: every year of his presidency Obama's administration has spent more as a percentage of GDP than any of his predecessors going back to 1946. Harry Truman was president then—and, in case you'd forgotten, he had just finished leading the country through World War II.

Even if Obama had any qualms about deficit spending—and there's no reason to believe that he does—he could still be reassured by the "moderates" and liberals in the mainstream media chorusing that all this deficit spending is really okay—beneficial, even. In *News-week*, for example, David Frum, a former Republican speechwriter who devotes his columns to being outraged by conservatives, wrote, "I know I forfeit my membership in respectable society when I say this, but I don't worry very much about the U.S. deficit and the U.S. debt."[31] Actually, the "respectable society" Frum travels in—the mainstream media—has never really worried much about debt to begin with. At the *New York Times*, influential columnist Paul Krugman wrote, "when people in D.C. talk about deficits and debt, by and large they have no idea what they're talking about—and the people who talk the most understand the least."[32] Krugman avers that "deficits are actually a good thing when the economy is deeply depressed, so deficit reduction should wait until the economy is stronger." Krugman is one of the nation's most passionate advocates of inflation, debt, and endless spending.

Then there is the *Washington Post*'s self-styled wizard of wonkery, Ezra Klein, who represents a popular new breed of pundit that believes the world can be comprehensively understood by generating an array of charts. He explained in a Bloomberg column that he was "not particularly worried about the budget deficit. In fact, of all the major problems the U.S. faces, I'm least worried about the deficit."[33] All the problems? Jeez. I'm not sure what that means, exactly, but accepting Klein's contention would mean that one of the *Washington Post*'s premiere columnists is more concerned about funding Elmo on PBS than he is about $16 trillion in national debt.

Even former President Bill Clinton, once the representative of the centrist wing of his party, a man who boasts incessantly about a debt-free federal government handed to him by an effective conservative Congress, explained during a campaign stop for the president in 2012 not to get too excited about the debt. (At *Business Insider*,

Joe Weisenthal, one of the Internet's most popular business writers, lambasted Clinton for even carrying a surplus. "If the government is in surplus, it means that the government is taking in more cash than it's spending, which is the opposite of stimulus,"[34] he explained.) And Robert Reich, the man who served as Secretary of Labor under Clinton, says: "I wish President Obama and the Democrats would explain to the nation that the federal budget deficit isn't the nation's major economic problem and deficit reduction shouldn't be our major goal."[35] Please explain! The president did just that—sort of—when he stopped in for a chat with David Letterman. He explained, "we don't have to worry about [the debt] short term." No, of course not. We'll only have to worry about it after he's out of office and the debt has ballooned to who knows how much bigger.

Per U.S. taxpayer, the level of debt now stands at more than $111,000. So when should I start worrying—or should I just assume that my kids can handle the problem, the way that the Democrats like to assume that "the wealthy" can foot every possible expense that they hang on the taxpayers? You'll notice that, according to liberal pundits and politicians, there's never a good time to trouble ourselves with these matters. Not really. When we're in periods of booming growth, the argument is that government can afford to spend more. When we're struggling through recessions, the government needs to spend more on "stimulus"—and to ensure that public sector workers keep their jobs while private sector firms get leaner.

To Democrats, spending cuts—unless they're targeted at the Pentagon—are always intrinsically immoral. (Although I'm not arguing that defense spending couldn't use a haircut, ironically it—unlike, say, green subsidies—may be one of the few ways government actually can create viable, private sector high-tech jobs in fields like aerospace and engineering.) Beyond Obama's dazzling propensity for squandering cash, it is vital to understand why the debt explosion can't be averted: it's because Obama and the Democrats have no interest in averting it. Obama's deficit spending wasn't caused by negligence or instituted as a short-term fix, a temporary necessity (as he sometimes likes to claim), or an unintended byproduct of some idealistic liberal policymaking. It is the ideal.

Spending is the very point of Obama's economic policy. Spending is how we fix the economy; it's how we spread prosperity; it's how we mete out fairness; it's the point of the entire project. Worrying about the deficit only stands in the way of instituting the tenets of an ethical society and putting the nation on the road to progress. Increasing revenue by broadening the tax base, or instituting a flattened tax rate, or reforming deductions, or using any other new ideas about collecting revenue, can be counterproductive because it would mean everyone would have to pay up for the promise of state-offered hope. Debt, on the other hand, demands nothing from most of us—for now, at least.

In some sense, all the debates in Washington regarding the specifics of spending and revenue are a sham. Budgets themselves are an endangered species. The Senate hasn't actually passed one since 2009. The Obama administration believes that a healthy economy—nay, a moral one—can only be judged by the size of its expenditures. Government spending is not a burden; it's a gift. It's a benefit. It's not just the big-ticket items either. Government spending on programs large and small improves our communal life, or so we're told.

Take U.S. Secretary of Agriculture Tom Vilsack, for example. He argued that the immense expansion of the food stamps program was not just to help the poor put food on the table. "You have to recognize," he said in the summer of 2011, "that it's also an economic stimulus," because "obviously, it's putting people to work."

Food stamps were, "exciting in terms of job growth."[36] Every dollar of this exciting food stamp spending, Vilsack claimed, generated $1.84 in terms of economic activity. "If people are able to buy a little more in the grocery store, someone has to stock it, package it, shelve it, process it, ship it. All of those are jobs. It's the most direct stimulus you can get in the economy during these tough times." This was Keynesian twaddle of the highest order, but it was deployed by nearly every Democrat and in nearly every case of welfare spending. (Even John Maynard Keynes, who believed in deficit spending to prop up economic growth, might have been appalled at the way his theory was used by spendthrift Democrats.) Common sense, in short supply in Washington, should tell us that if we want real economic growth we should favor expanding businesses that create more wealth and open up new jobs, not a goliath federal government shaking down taxpayers in an effort to drive food stamp traffic to prop up jobs at the local 24-hour superstore. But of course, if we left economic growth to the private sector, what would bureaucrats do? What would the secretary of agriculture do? How could they stimulate the economy and claim to be creating jobs and saving the poor from starvation (while Michelle Obama saves them from obesity)? To Democrats, every dollar government spends further stimulates the economy. If this were true, why wouldn't we hand out money to everyone who asks?

Oh wait…

Those in the administration argued that unemployment itself could generate economic activity. According to the Obama administration, extending unemployment benefits generates $1.61 for every dollar spent. By this logic, the economy can actually profit from unemployment if the government sends out enough checks. In fact, every dollar from an unemployment check helps the economy 61 percent more than every after-tax dollar that you earn in the private sector and spend on food and clothing and at the hardware store. Isn't that amazing? It's a wonder we haven't seen an explosion of the GDP during the Obama years.

When a *Wall Street Journal* reporter asked the White House press secretary Jay Carney to explain this rather curious assertion, he had the temerity to answer, "Oh, uh, it is by, um, I would expect a reporter from *The Wall Street Journal* would know this as part of the entrance exam," going on to say, "There are few other ways that can directly put money into the economy than applying unemployment insurance. It is one of the most direct ways to infuse money directly into the economy because people who are unemployed and obviously aren't running a paycheck are going to spend the money that they get. They're not going to save it, they're going to spend it. And with unemployment insurance, that way, the money goes directly back into the economy, dollar for dollar virtually."[37]

The entrance exam to Obama U, perhaps. And, actually, Jay, there are *countless* ways to infuse money directly into the economy—and the Obama administration has figured out nearly every conceivable one. Here's how that worked out. During the Obama recovery, the average real GDP growth has been less than half the historical average, just over 2 percent. Of the past 11 national recoveries, Obama spearheaded by far the weakest. George H. W. Bush, George W. Bush, Carter, Clinton, Eisenhower, Ford, Johnson, Kennedy, Nixon, Reagan, and Truman all saw stronger economic recoveries than Obama. None of them, as far as I can tell, ever made an argument that food stamps and unemployment benefits were policies that helped recovery, and all of them saw a much stronger bounce back. It's not that we haven't tried similar stimulus programs before—though far smaller ones— but that they never worked. In their book *The End of Prosperity*, economist Arthur Laffer and the *Wall Street Journal*'s Stephen Moore revisit 2001, when George W. Bush larded his tax cut plan with Keynesian-style stimulus after the dot-com bubble burst. Rebate checks were sent to 95 million people who filed tax returns. As Ryan Dwyer, a fellow with the National Review Institute, points out, "This approach faltered, not just because Americans opted to save their rebates, but because it neglected the importance of business investment to overall growth. Predictably, the economy lagged and government revenues stagnated. What the United States needed then (and needs now) was to stimulate investment, not consumption."[38]

Remember, as well, that a trillion-dollar yearly deficit, a habit with the Obama administration, is itself a yearly stimulus plan (larger than the original 2009 stimulus, actually). Its success, like the success of other stimulus plans, can be measured in the creation of gargantuan new debt rather than jobs or prosperity. Liberals believe the private sector is driven by greed, generates inequality, and is crassly narrow-minded compared to the broad perspective that the experts in Washington take. Technocrats, unlike the barbarians of a capitalistic meritocracy, take the best interests of the citizenry into consideration. Our friend Paul Krugman once explained, "I actually have a serious proposal which is that we have to get a bunch of scientists to tell us that we're facing a threatened alien invasion, and in order to be prepared for that alien invasion we have to do things like build high-speed rail. And then, once we've recovered, we can say, 'Look, there were no aliens.'" Anything to spend more taxpayer dollars on projects for bureaucrats and jobs for unionized public employees.

Long ago, the economist Frederic Bastiat exposed the economic fallacy embraced by the likes of Krugman and the Obama administration. In Bastiat's famous parable of the broken window, a shopkeeper's son breaks a pane of glass. The father, lucky guy, will now have to pay to replace the glass and this will, naturally, help generate economic growth because the local unionized glazier will be employed to fix the window. The glazier will then spend his earnings on some local organic groceries, and so on and so forth. Bastiat points out that by smashing his window, the man's son has reduced his father's wealth and left him holding the bag. The father will not be able to purchase his own new shoes or his own gas-guzzling car. Thus, the broken window might help the glazier, but at the same time, it robs other industries and reduces the amount being spent on other goods. So the lesson for today is this: if you're earning a living in the private sector, think of yourself as the shopkeeper, and the Obama administration as a gang of thugs running down the street breaking all your windows—staying long enough to lecture you on how all the glass strewn across your shop will help stimulate the collective economy.

Politics = Doom

Even more alarming than impending space invasions (and, to be perfectly fair, preparing for imaginary alien attacks is likely as productive as focusing on windmills and Volts), is how progressives have also inverted what was once considered conventional thinking on spending. There was a time not that long ago when small sacrifices might have sufficed to avert disasters—small sacrifices that sounded precariously like common sense: cutting spending when you're spending more than you take in, for instance. Today, alas, we're told that such ideas are half-baked, when they're not radical or even destructive. Obama Democrats, although politically triumphant, have staked out a rather cramped ideological corner, where even proposals for spending slowdowns—forget about cuts that will never happen—are the work of nihilists and anarchists and Republican obstructionists at war with the future. The fact is, though, that the future is coming, it is going to hand us a very large bill, and the Democrats seem supremely confident that they're going to find someone else to pay for it.

Through all the economic turmoil of Obama's first four years, one thing was constant: the drumbeat that the nation will rise or fall depending on how much it can tax the wealthy—and the higher the tax rates, the better. The president spent four years arguing that Bush-era top marginal tax rates were why the country was trillions of dollars in debt. That's right—allowing earners to keep more of their earnings is bad for the country. He also blamed the recession on tax cuts. He blamed slow economic growth on tax cuts. He blamed the plight of the deteriorating middle class on tax cuts. Yet, according to projections of the Congressional Budget Office, revenue-wise, reverting to Clinton-era tax rates on the rich would amount to, perhaps—if a tax hike doesn't end up dampening economic growth even further—around $824 billion in revenue over the next decade. In other words, less than one year of deficit spending by the administration.[39] That's it. To be fair, Democrats had also been fighting for an additional millionaire "Buffett" tax, which might raise—maybe—$47 billion over the next decade, or less than $5 billion a year, or around half a workday of the federal government's budget.[40] So there's that.

The Democrats keep pretending that the rich can pay for our spending, and it's a popular idea. According to an ABC News/*Washington Post* poll conducted in November 2012, raising taxes on incomes of more than $250,000 a year was supported by 73 percent of Democrats, 63 percent of independents, and even 39 percent of Republicans. If you want to see how big government has corrupted the morality of the American people, you don't need to point fingers at single moms on welfare; you could just as well indict the majority of the American people who think it is perfectly "fair" that other people should pay for their stuff—whatever stuff they get, or think they get, from the federal government.

Things are, it should be noted, already more than "fair." Not only do the rich pony up the preponderance of federal income tax, but, as the *Wall Street Journal* recently reported, the United States is more dependent on wealthy taxpayers than are most socialized economies of Europe. Washington gets "45 percent of its total taxes from the top 10 percent of tax filers, whereas the international average in industrialized nations is 32 percent."[41]

Okay, so punitive tax rates on the rich are popular. Not surprising. But does anyone really believe that—even if such tax policies did generate new tax revenues—Obama would use that money to reduce the debt? Well, a few of you, I suppose, do believe, although the majority knows better. A new Public Notice poll found that the majority of men (61 percent), women (53 percent), and independents (60 percent) believe that the president would use newfound money to increase spending rather than to cut deficits. The rest were still living in a fantasy. But this also brings to mind a question: If the majority of independents know the money will just fund Obama's free-spending ways and make the deficit worse, why do the majority of independents support raising taxes on the rich?

One reason, no doubt, is the media's lack of equally critical coverage. When former vice presidential candidate Paul Ryan wrote his budget, called "The Path to Prosperity" (there were two versions), he offered voters a conservative approach to budgeting that, at the very least, took debt seriously. He took the budget seriously. He offered some accountability and reform. So how did the White House—a White House that offered no detailed plan to cut debt—respond? "The House budget once again fails the test of balance, fairness, and shared responsibility. It would shower the wealthiest few Americans with an average tax cut of at least $150,000, while preserving taxpayer giveaways to oil companies and breaks for Wall Street hedge fund managers."[42]

Basically, this is—almost verbatim—the left's response to every budget proposal that doesn't jack up tax rates. Not only are such vacuous populist platitudes par for the course over the past four years but, sad to say, this was the kind of rhetoric that helped Obama win reelection. Thus, it's probably a waste of time to point out how little of the White House's statement was true. After all, no matter what the topic is, or how critical the consequences may be for the country, the White House is going to claim that the Republicans want to reform Social Security by pushing the elderly off a cliff; that the GOP doesn't feel the pain of the middle class, which can only be assuaged by redirecting the ill-gotten gains of the rich; that Republicans are troglodytes who want to wage war on women by taking them back to the dark days before there were taxpayer-funded condoms, morning-after pills, and abortions; and that the GOP cares about nobody but Daddy Warbucks, who by investing or spending his vast wealth is obviously doing far less good for the economy than if he turned it over to the bureaucrats in Washington who really know what to do with it.

The Obama administration was never serious about cutting debt, and class-based scaremongering was the best way to avoid having to negotiate in good faith. Tax rate hikes, they like; giant new government programs like Obamacare are the administration's signature; talk about debt reduction is a non-starter. Paul Ryan's plan to roll back discretionary federal spending to 2008 levels is, to the liberal establishment, radical. But adding $11 trillion to the national debt,[43] as Obama's first proposed budget in 2011 did (a budget that not a single elected official, Democrat or Republican, voted for; in the Senate it lost 97–0[44]), is just levelheaded policy. Search I did, but I couldn't find a single reporter who challenged the president on it. Hardly a newspaper or any mainstream news outlet mentioned how full-on crazy *that* was—conceivably, they didn't really find it extreme at all.

And when the president carved out $700 billion from Medicare as seed money for a new trillion-dollar health care insurance entitlement project that will cost more than we can possibly calculate, one would have thought it was a completely rational way for government to operate. Yet when Ryan proposes similar cuts to extend the life of Medicare, a program that—unlike Obamacare—Americans favored, he was portrayed as a granny killer. When Paul Ryan injected the same reactionary idea into Medicare that the average American struggles with every day as he heads out into the marketplace to buy food or furniture or a phone—that is, offering a slightly more market-based *option* for people 55 and younger—Democrats and editorial boards around the nation treated it as if it were the vilest form of social Darwinism.

Ryan's budget was not a plan for severely shrinking the federal government. In fact, his budget showed spending increasing every year for ten straight years. He was trying to recapture the baseline spending that was hiked when we passed that "one-time" stimulus plan. If that sort of plan is considered radical in Washington, then just how are we ever going to have a budget that comes anywhere close to reducing our federal debt, rather than perpetually ratcheting it up?

It really is discouraging to read or hear the sort of half-baked rhetoric Obama gets away with. It's really incredible to think about what passes as conventional thinking these days. The president claimed the Republicans wanted to reinstitute the policies that were responsible for getting us into this "mess" in the first place. Voters agreed. But what on earth does a plan that allows seniors—ten years from now—to use their own Medicare dollars to take part in private plans or stick with the traditional government-run system have to do with the current recession? What does reforming the tax code, flattening it, and broadening the base have to do with recreating subprime mortgages and a housing bubble? And if we get right down to it, wasn't it the Democrat-protected government whiz kids at Fannie Mae and Freddie Mac who helped drive the whole mortgage catastrophe? And while we're at it, wasn't *debt* a big part of the problem leading to the financial crisis; and who is the biggest debtor of them all, do you think?

In 2012, a Gallup poll claimed that 45 percent of Americans favored reducing the federal deficit with an equal balance of tax increases and spending cuts—up from 32 percent from the year before.[45] Americans like a balanced approach to problems. Or so we say. Yet, after the Obama victory in November 2012, Republicans quickly conceded huge swaths of their argument for a balanced approach. Both House Speaker John Boehner and Senate Minority Leader Mitch McConnell immediately surrendered to the idea that "revenue" should drive our focus rather than unsustainable "spending" when dealing with impending budgetary problems.

Obama often claimed that his top concern after the election was averting a fiscal cliff—shorthand, as I'm sure you know, for the array of tax increases and automatic spending that would have automatically kicked in at the beginning of 2013. He was far more concerned about seeing tax rates on the rich rise, though he was magnanimously flexible on the details. The president claimed to be open to all "new ideas" as long as those ideas "raise revenue, maintain progressivity, make sure the middle class isn't getting hit, and encourage growth."[46] In Obama's Washington, this is called "compromise." Obama also claimed to be "very eager" to reform the tax code and believed that entitlements such as Medicare and Social Security needed a "serious look," but gave absolutely no hint on how he would move forward. He was so eager to deal with this that for four years—two of them with Democrats in complete power—he hadn't offered a single substantive agenda item that might deal with any of it. Who knows? Maybe he was just waiting for the second term, right?

Hey, you can't put a limit on a dream, can you? In a 2012 interview with Bloomberg's Al Hunt, Treasury Secretary Timothy Geithner was asked, "Do you agree with Alan Greenspan that we ought to just eliminate the debt ceiling?"

"Oh, absolutely." he replied.[47]

The debt ceiling, a legal restriction on the amount of money the U.S. government can borrow, is a mechanism with which many Americans are too familiar these days. Hypothetically, the debt ceiling is intended to do the obvious. Congressional action is required to increase this debt ceiling—which also acts to constantly remind voters of how irresponsible their government has been—so Geithner, quite naturally, would like to throw the entire idea into the garbage along with other antiquated notions of limited government.

Today, the administration might favor eliminating any constraints on debt, but Obama argued long ago that raising America's debt limit was a sign of failed leadership, a signal, he claimed, that the U.S. government could not pay its own bills and that we were dependent on the assistance of foreigners to fund our "reckless" fiscal policies.[48] Those were the impetuous days of 2006, when Democrats railed against increasing the debt ceiling because Bush was "spending" money on unpleasant things like war and tax cuts. Today we have the infrastructure of a socialized health care system to implement, we have welfare programs to expand and entitlement reforms to ignore, and debt ceilings are an inconvenience. Nevertheless, most Americans, at least according to a CBS News/*New York Times* poll conducted a few years ago, are not only fans of the debt ceiling but oppose raising it. Just 27 percent think it should be increased, while 63 percent oppose doing so—a number encompassing 64 percent of independents and 48 percent of Democrats.[49]

Still, there are two problems with the debt ceiling. The first is that it doesn't really exist. Not really. The debt ceiling is like the speed limit on an interstate highway—a theoretical limit, at best. And every time Washington sets a new cap, it does so knowing full well that another hike will be needed soon enough and that they'll get it without much of a fuss. Since 1962, the debt ceiling has been raised 75 times—11 times since 2001 (not counting the one or two times the cap hikes have been instituted since the writing of this sentence).[50]

The second problem is that if the ceiling were not adjusted, the United States would be sucked into a cycle of default, unable to pay its debts. The United States, of course, will not default, regardless of who happens to be in charge. So we lift and lift. There really is no choice.

Debt ceiling negotiations, though, are one of the few moments where an opportunity to cut deals on future spending arises. During the last four years we witnessed a couple of bizarre debates on the topic, followed by a couple of predictable Republican defeats. What makes these debates over raising the cap unlike the others is that Democrats have taken to arguing that we should do away with debt limits altogether; they argue, in essence, that limits on debt, rather than debt itself, is the predicament. Common sense might contradict that, but if you believe that government spending is what drives economic growth, progress, and right moral action and thinking, then it makes perfect sense.

During one fight over the debt threshold, White House Press Secretary Jay Carney accused Republicans of engaging in criminal behavior. "It is simply not acceptable to hold the American and global economy hostage to one party's political ideology," he said. The White House used this formulation endlessly. What was he talking about? Wasn't debt holding us hostage? Spending cuts to make a dent in deficit spending was "ideology" rather than, say, prudence or account-ability? The debt ceiling at the time was at nearly $15 trillion dollars. The Obama administration lifted it to $16.4 trillion. That barely lasted until the 2012 presidential election, with Treasury Secretary Timothy Geithner using his "policy tools," as he called them, to keep the debt ceiling debate from derailing Obama's bid for a second term.[51]

Geithner, actually, is the impeccable representative of an Obama technocrat—the type of person who can tell you that a dollar of spending will generate 1.61 dollars of economic activity with assur-ance and a smile. Indeed, the administration likes to pretend that all the really smart people back its policies. Obama liked to claim, for instance, that "every economist, from the left and the right, has said, because of the Recovery Act, what we've started to see is at least a couple of million jobs that have either been created or would have been lost."[52] Well, actually, plenty of economists disagreed with Obama. The libertarian Cato Institute quickly ran ads featuring 200 economists who thought massive government spending to stimulate the economy was a bad idea.

But the belief that technocratic experts can guide the economy from Washington is a pillar of Obama administration thinking. Example A might be Christina Romer, former chairwoman of Presi-dent Barack Obama's Council of Economic Advisers and one of the chief architects of the failed stimulus plan—and the entire economic agenda of the administration. In 2009, Romer and another economist, Jared Bernstein, predicted rather famously—in graph form so that even not-so-bright journalists like myself could comprehend the problem—that an "unprecedented and pragmatic" $800 billion stimulus would keep the unemployment rate at less than 8 percent moving forward. Likewise, she claimed that the unemployment rate would plunge to 5.6 percent by the end of Obama's first term. In reality, Obama's first stint ended with unemployment at 7.9 percent (and it was probably a lot worse than it seemed with an ever-shrinking labor force), and unemployment peaked at over 10 percent.

Romer retreated back to academia, where the theoretic powers of predicting the future are really valued. Her farewell remarks, as Dana Milbank of the *Washington Post* reported, were littered with phrases such as "economists don't fully understand why" and "almost all analysts were surprised," and so on and so forth, about Obama's stimulus failure. It was something they "failed to anticipate." Funny, because it was quite the turnaround from the certitude she displayed when offering her predictions and laying out plans for the spending of $800 billion taxpayer dollars. But the fact is, you can find an economist to tell you anything. And this administration found tons to tell them exactly what they wanted to hear.

Romer did offer us another nugget about how "economists" and other levelheaded experts in the White House think about debt. "Concern about the deficit," she explained once, discussing extending unemployment benefits (which you will remember other "economists" have told us is a real prosperity generator), "cannot be an excuse for leaving unemployed workers to suffer." You know, that doesn't sound especially scientific to me. It sounds empathetic (perhaps) and highly political. How does suffering fit into an economist's calculations, one wonders? Surely some economists believe that extending unemployment benefits is a disincentive to finding a new job—and thus creates more suffering? Obviously there is legitimate disagreement among social scientists on which policy is best in trying to achieve our goals. The administration did their best to try and create the illusion that there is near unanimity among economists, which, of course, is a lie. Certainly, no one can question the intellectual talent of Romer—but in judging the academic heavyweights around Obama, we always should remember Woody Allen's truism: "That's one thing about intellectuals: they've proved that you can be absolutely brilliant and have no idea what's going on."

Default, Inflation, or Austerity—if We're Lucky

What is the ultimate effect of massive federal debt? Well, for one thing, it corrodes what I suppose we now have to consider an antiquated ideal: economic liberty. In the shorter term, high debt inevitably means higher taxes and that means bigger government, which continues this inescapable cycle.

Then there is a little matter of economic calamity.

A quick reminder: the CBO reports that entitlement programs and interest on debt will consume all the revenues going into the budget by 2025. As I do with all events that I may still be alive for, I categorize this as "not that far off."

The future we face is not just one of utterly crippling taxes, though those are coming too. To pay off the debt—not to mention the interest on that debt—will mean dramatic cuts in programs across the board. Liberals might not mind too much if the Pentagon goes into mothballs, but what they haven't told you is that the fiscal disaster they've laid out for us means inevitable cuts to Social Security and Medicare benefits.

For years we've heard about "unsustainable" entitlement programs. We'll find out what that really means when they go bust.

Even today, at least in a small way, we can see this future playing out in the states. Illinois, the state that elected Obama to the Senate, is a good example. As the *New York Times* recently noted, the state was compelled to "plug budget holes, pay overdue bills, and put money into its mismanaged pension funds. And for the people who live there, this has resulted in decrepit commuter trains and buses, thousands of unsound bridges, 200 hazardous dams and one of the most inequitable public school systems in America."[53] The future for Illinois: more tax increases, more cuts in education and transportation, and more layoffs. It'll be far worse when the federal government has to follow the same course.

For the first time in American history, America is seen as a bit of a credit risk. Moody's, for one, cut its outlook on U.S. debt to "negative," a move that likely signaled future downgrades. Standard & Poor's stripped the United States of its "AAA" rating on its bonds. Fitch Ratings issued a warning of a potential downgrade. The only reason the United States has been able to continue borrowing at very low rates is because U.S. government bonds are still ranked higher than European ones, given their own debt crises. But that will be scant comfort in the future. As Senator Tom Coburn, one of the leading voices of reason in the Senate on debt, told CBS, "We're going to get another downgrade. I can tell you right now. You can have a great legal case for suing the rating agencies for not downgrading us again because we have not demonstrated the political will to solve the problems."[54] You can say that again.

But focusing on our future of high taxes, rising interest rates, and slashed government programs is almost to miss the main point, which is that debt is going to destroy our standard of living by tanking the economy. As economists Jason J. Fichtner and Jakina R. Debnam argue in their paper, "Reducing Debt and Other Measures for Improving U.S. Competitiveness," massive government debt destabilizes economies by crowding out private investment and raising costs to private businesses. They lay it out this way:[55]

- The current level of debt sits at more than $16 trillion.
- Because of this, the government is forced to redirect resources from productive activities to paying its debt.
- Furthermore, when the government turns to borrowing, interest rates go up on private businesses.
- As a result, profits and overall growth decline, which hurts the economy.
- Additionally, high levels of debt create uncertainty about the appropriate tax levels needed to service the debt as well as the potential for inflation, which hurts overall productivity and growth.

There are only three possible ways of escaping a jarring showdown with debt, listed below.

One: Massive Inflation

The Democrats' plan for debt is taken, knowingly or not, from Dionysius, the first supreme military commander and dictator of Syracuse in the fourth century B.C. No doubt looking to fund much-needed populist infrastructure projects, he began to subsidize short-term needs by borrowing copious amounts of gold from various folks around town. He got carried away with the borrowing, as governments tend to do, and was unable to repay his loans. He came up with an ingenious solution. As the story goes, he confiscated all the gold coins he could and changed the denomination from "1 drachma" to read "2 drachma" and repaid everyone. Today this can be called "Fed policy."

Monetary policy is a complex and mystical business—it also ties in seamlessly with the administration's focus on flooding the economy with money. "It is very important to keep politics out of monetary policy,"[56] Tim Geithner explained in an interview with Bloomberg Television not long ago. "You want to be very careful not to take steps that hurt our credibility." Political or not, perhaps we've allowed the power of the Federal Reserve System to go unchallenged for too long? Have we given too much deference to gurus who speak in Fiscal Koans rather than English and who are presumed to be infallible, with no need of oversight or accountability? Maybe it's time to re-examine the Fed's role, as Ron Paul has urged for years. Under Obama the supposedly apolitical Fed has seemed plenty political.

Not long ago it began a third round of "quantitative easing"— colloquially known as QE3, or "printing loads of money and giving it to big banks that follow the administration's instructions"—as if the Obama administration hadn't spent enough. The second round of quantitative easing, good old QE2, had already dropped another $600 billion into the economy even though the first round of more than $1 trillion failed to do much of anything. In fact, it is estimated that more than $3 trillion has been thrown into the economic mix since we started fixing the recession. By the time QE3 came, a few months before Election Day, the Fed promised to spend $40 billion a month on mortgage-backed securities with no set date to end those purchases. Now the spigot is open for good.

This is not legislation but it is more spending and it devalues our economy. The Fed, I think it's fair to say, was trying to bail out the Washington establishment and specifically the Obama administration. During the first four years of Obama, we have had three rounds of quantitative easing, a trillion dollar stimulus, even the Fed's "Operation Twist" in the bond market, and trillion-dollar-a-year deficits—and the economy has still stalled. You think maybe the Obama plan isn't working?

Dr. Esmael Adibi, Director of the A. Gary Anderson Center for Economic Research at Chapman University, told me that he believes QE3 was completely unnecessary. "It is not going to help the economy. If the goal is to create jobs it's not going to do much. If the goal is to run up stock prices then maybe it will work in the short term. But, in the end, earnings are what is important, and they are based on the real economy." Adibi believes the goal is to pump up the markets. "If the stock market does well, it will improve consumer confidence, you'll feel better about your retirement plan and portfolio and that, they hope, will stimulate the economy."

Feeling good is, no doubt, important. But many economists argue that this kind of policy has the potential to feed economic bubbles, distort trade, push nations to engage in competing devaluations, cause long-term inflation at home, and transform your dollar into something…well, less.

The Fed has run out of tools. It has exhausted its ability to act beyond printing money. And act it does, even though many economists argue that it is worry about the Obama administration's spending policies and debt, rather than liquidity, that's driving our economic troubles.

The Fed has aligned itself ideologically with the administration and it is making some of the most important policy decisions in the nation. So why shouldn't we politicize the bank? Politics is the best way for us to sift through these concerns. In no other sphere of public policymaking is anyone inoculated from accountability like this—

except perhaps in the White House. A public debate on inflation could be a useful exercise.

Two: Massive Economic Boom

It is plausible—though barely, at this point, considering how hostile Obama is towards free enterprise—that some unforeseen technological advancement will spur a huge economic boom and save us from the inevitable. To work, it would have to be far bigger than the tech boom of the 1990s. But given the huge swath of economic regulation Obama has spun over the economy, our entrepreneurs barely have enough room to breathe, let alone to light a roaring economic fire.

Or—and this is probably our best chance—we could have an energy production explosion that will carry the entire economy. But as we all know, the Obama administration is no friend of the productive energy sector. It only likes its subsidized green projects. So the administration might easily kill an energy-based recovery.

So what's left?

Three: Pray

CHAPTER FOUR

IDENTITY CRISIS

*"Only a complete moral idiot can believe for an instant
that we are fighting against the wretched of the earth.
We are fighting, as I said before, against the scum of the earth."*
—CHRISTOPHER HITCHENS, *BOSTON GLOBE*, SEPTEMBER 8, 2002

*"The moment you give up your principles, and your values, y
ou are dead, your culture is dead, your civilisation is dead. Period."*
—ORIANA FALLACI, *WALL STREET JOURNAL*, JUNE 23, 2005

In the twentieth century, the United States was provoked into entering two World Wars in order to make the world "safe for democracy." In the Cold War, the distinction between the United States as the leader of the free world and the Communist bloc as a dictatorial regime was pretty stark. In the so-called "war on terror"—really a war against radical Islamists seeking a global caliphate—George W. Bush tried to draw a firm line dividing "us" from "them."

Barack Obama, however, has tossed away such certainties. To him, America is no shining city on a hill. We are not exceptional. We are no better than any other country and have no right to sit in judgment.

And as for American interests? America's chief interest, under the Obama administration, appears to be offering appeasement to America's enemies, giving support to revolutionaries seeking to overthrow at least tepidly pro-Western autocrats (in Tunisia and Egypt) or former enemies who didn't want to go the way of Saddam Hussein (Muammar Gaddafi in Libya), and ignoring popular movements against our enemies (as in the attempted Green Revolution in Iran) whose success might have helped stave off future headaches (such as a nuclear Iran). To put it mildly, Obama's foreign policy seems adrift from our interests, and from the principles for which we used to stand.

Will You Love Us When We're Sorry?

Actually, do we stand for anything anymore? Sometimes it's hard to say. More than any specific initiative on foreign policy Barack Obama has undertaken, the values he projected should have been most disconcerting to us. The vacuous rhetoric, the tolerance of illiberal ideology, the feigned humility, and the occasional acts of self-flagellation certainly haven't made us safer. Appeasement has corroded our standing in the world and is threatening our future.

It started with the bowing thing. Surely it was weird—and for some of you, probably a tad humiliating—to witness the president of the United States bending at the waist to theocrats like King Abdullah of Saudi Arabia[1] or royalty like Japan's Emperor Akihito.[2] It was merely protocol, argued the president's defenders. Maybe. As Pamela Eyring, the president of The Protocol School of Washington, told Fox News, there are no "hard-and-fast" rules on how a president should behave, although she noted, "When you're representing the United States of America, everything speaks…on behalf of our country. It's a visual. It shows more of a subservient look."[3] It would be hard to imagine President Truman bowing to the Emperor Hirohito or to a Saudi theocrat. But America has changed—as has the Democratic Party.

Then there were the apologies. Mitt Romney, during his failed presidential campaign, criticized Obama's international "apology tour" and Obama's comment during the 2008 campaign calling America an international bully. "No, Mr. President. America has freed other nations from dictators," Romney retorted.[4] Obama must have felt the heat. He vowed at the 113th annual National Convention of the Veterans of Foreign Wars in Reno, Nevada, that the United States "will never apologize." And he added, "Just as you protected America, we're going to pass our country to the next generation, stronger and safer and more respected in the world."[5]

That remains unlikely.

But Romney's mention of the "apology tour" had this effect—it pushed the mainstream media to defend its favorite. Obama responded during a debate by claiming, "every reporter who's looked at it, Governor, has said this is not true." And sure enough, an army of news media "fact-checkers" tried to deny that Obama's apology tour was anything more than astute statesmanship and nothing like Romney's scurrilous accusation that the president of the United States had gone bowing and scraping around the world. CNN reported that the president had never actually used the word "apology" or "sorry." ABC News' Senior Political Correspondent Jonathan Karl likewise reported that the president had never issued a formal apology to any nation, and went on to explain, "The President didn't apologize for America. He did acknowledge some mistakes that the United States had made, but there's no way you could really call it 'an apology tour.'"[6]

Why, yes, Mr. Karl, we can. So let's get a bit of housekeeping out of the way and define our terms: my dictionary says that "apology" means, among other things, "an admission of error or discourtesy accompanied by an expression of regret." By that definition, Obama has been apologizing for the United States since he became president. No president, in fact—not even Jimmy Carter—has been so insistent on making amends for America's previous behavior.

Obama had been in office only five months when he jetted off to Egypt to make amends to the Muslim world. On June 4, 2009, he delivered a platitude-filled lecture at Cairo University,[7] the crux of which was that we are all citizens of the world with only negligible differences between East and West, Christianity and Islam. We, in the West, certainly do not own the high moral ground. Also, we're sorry. We were wrong. Often.

Obama promised a new beginning between the United States and the world's Muslims, a new relationship based on "mutual interest and mutual respect" and "upon the truth that America and Islam are not exclusive, and need not be in competition." Obama claimed his address was an effort to "speak the truth" about our nation's relationship with the Muslim world—implying, of course, that we had been lying up to this point. For years we had been driven by crass cowboyism rather than tolerance. Now we would be humble. A few times audience members called out "we love you" and the speech ended, you won't be surprised, with a standing ovation.

As part of Obama's process of turning over a new leaf with the Islamic world, the United States stopped talking about Islamist terrorism, referring instead to "man-caused disasters." Janet Napolitano, President Obama's Homeland Security secretary, explained in an interview with Der Spiegel that the rhetorical shift "demonstrates that we want to move away from the politics of fear toward a policy of being prepared for all risks that can occur."[8] It is a matter of faith in the Obama administration that when terrorists attempt to blow up cars in Times Square or kill soldiers at Fort Hood, America is not threatened by Islamism, but merely by rogue individuals. In fact, rather than seeing as an example of Islamist terrorism the Fort Hood shooting of November 5, 2009, which a known radical Muslim committed, the administration used it to celebrate diversity. Army Chief of Staff General George Casey said, "Our diversity, not only in our Army, but in our country, is a strength. And as horrific as this tragedy was, if our diversity becomes a casualty, I think that's worse." President Obama also celebrated diversity in his radio address the Saturday after the shootings.[9]

Diversity as our strength is a liberal cliché. Another liberal cliché is that George W. Bush was an ignoramus who poisoned our relationship with the Muslim world—no matter how much Bush promoted the idea that Islam is a religion of peace. Obama went to Cairo to seek forgiveness for the sins of George W. Bush, and for his almost equally ignorant American predecessors. But whatever one makes of the wars in Afghanistan and Iraq, following the September 11, 2001, terrorist attacks on this country, it is an undeniable fact that American military action, which President Bush initiated, liberated two oppressed Muslim countries from tyrannical regimes—whether one considers them acts of foreign policy prudence or wasteful expenditures of American lives and treasure. The United States did so at enormous cost to itself, and with the best of intentions, any sane observer would have to note, trying to establish two peaceful Islamic democracies that respected the rights of women (in Afghanistan) and of different tribal, ethnic, and religious groups (in Iraq)—even if the execution was not always perfect, even if enormous mistakes were made, and even if there were consequences American planners did not foresee (such as the plight of Iraqi Christians). The United States, in fact, has a not inconsiderable record of trying to protect Muslims—in Bosnia during the Balkan wars, in Kuwait against Iraqi invasion, in Somalia, and elsewhere.

But rather than focusing on what America has done for Muslims, and for the world, as a generous country, Obama prefers to talk to foreign audiences about America's litany of sins and about how we're no better than any other country. Speaking before the Turkish Parliament on April 6, 2009, Obama said, "Another issue that confronts all democracies as they move to the future is how we deal with the past. The United States is still working through some of our own darker periods in our history. Facing the Washington Monument that I spoke of is a memorial of Abraham Lincoln, the man who freed those who were enslaved even after Washington led our Revolution. Our country still struggles with the legacies of slavery and segregation, the past treatment of Native Americans," said the first African American president, a man who had easily triumphed in both campaigns against wealthy white men, despite his own lack of experience in the first round and a completely failed domestic record in the second.[10]

Obama believes, and formulates this conviction to foreign audiences, that the United States had no moral standing to lecture anyone. Turkey might be the nation that perpetrated the Armenian Genocide, the first real holocaust of the twentieth century; it may have systematically raped and plundered the Greek Cypriots; it may still oppress the Kurdish minority with Turkey—but really, we're no better. And part of being "no better" means not judging, which is why the administration is so painfully reluctant to link the words "terrorist" and "Islamist" or why the United States has preferred to "lead from behind" in North Africa and the Middle East. It's also why, when the president was given a chance to fulfill a 2008 campaign promise and acknowledge the genocide of 1.5 million Christian Armenians by

Turks, he instead did everything he could to block the resolution in the United Nations. The president did make good, however, on an apology to Native Americans (in 2010), because it's never too late to say you're sorry—again—if you're the United States. Obama signed a resolution that was "finally recognizing the sad and painful chapters in our shared history—a history too often marred by broken promises and grave injustices against the First Americans."[11] "Hopefully," the statement by Congress read, we can "move toward a brighter future where all the people of this land live reconciled as brothers and sisters, and harmoniously steward and protect this land together."

Imperfect as we are—and no one is arguing that the United States is without blemish—surely the president believes our institutions, goals, principles, and system of government are the finest anywhere. Surely the president, who swore to defend the Constitution, believes this unequivocally? Actually, not so surely. In 2001, Obama explained that the Constitution is "an imperfect document, and I think it is a document that reflects some deep flaws...I think we can say that the Constitution reflected an enormous blind spot in this culture that carries on until this day, and that the Framers had that same blind spot. I don't think the two views are contradictory, to say that it was a remarkable political document that paved the way for where we are now, and to say that it also reflected the fundamental flaw of this country that continues to this day."[12] Obama was referring in particular to slavery, but he left open the assumption that it was not the only flaw of the Constitution.

You might also remember how Obama, early in his presidency, told a French reporter, "I believe in American exceptionalism, just as I suspect that the Brits believe in British exceptionalism, and the Greeks believe in Greek exceptionalism."[13] So we're not all that exceptional or, perhaps we're all exceptional. Patriotism is like a provincial loyalty one might have for the Yankees or Phillies or the Toledo Mud Hens. The idea that the United States is a beacon to the world, the shining city on the hill, and the last best hope for man—all those foundational ideas about America that should bind us together no matter what other political beliefs we hold—is not exactly Obama's view. Instead, we're a deeply flawed country that needs a lot of work—and thank goodness he's in the White House to do it.

Obama himself is not exceptional in taking this view—it's the view of many liberals who, like Obama, cannot bring themselves to praise their own country without repudiations. Liberals have long scoffed at the notion of American moral superiority. When the president was taking some mild heat for his remarks on exceptionalism, left-wing columnist Michael Kinsley wrote a piece titled, "U.S. is not greatest country ever,"[14] in which he mocked those who traffic in exceptionalism. Daily Beast/*Newsweek* columnist Peter Beinart— once editor for the liberal *New Republic*—claimed that the GOP was enabling the "lunatic notion" of American exceptionalism.[15] The American story, in the progressive view, is not of a land of opportunity graced by God, but really the story of liberals and big government trying to exorcise the enduring American sins of racism, sexism, homophobia, and triumphalism. We are no better than anyone else; in fact our very power and success has made us, if anything, worse than other countries, because it has made us arrogant, which is why Obama is always so eager to pin culpability for nearly all the world's problems on the United States.

When visiting Strasbourg, France, in April 2009, Obama confessed to a European audience, "In America, there's a failure to appreciate Europe's leading role in the world. Instead of celebrating your dynamic union and seeking to partner with you to meet common challenges, there have been times where America's shown arrogance and been dismissive, even derisive."[16] Actually, if anything, the United States has bent over backwards to encourage the European Union, not to mention (as American veterans might remember) fighting in two world wars and a Cold War to restore and keep the peace in Europe, not to mention rebuilding Europe with the Marshall Plan. But it suits liberals to think of their fellow Americans as arrogant rubes who lack the sophistication and taste for socialism that Europeans have. And when it comes to lessons in arrogant and dismissive attitudes, you can't do better than to talk to Europeans about America.

According to the Pew Global Attitudes Project, for example, most Europeans are contemptuous of American-style democracy. Italy is the only European country, actually, where a majority (58 percent) admired our form of government. What about American-style capitalism? Only around 26 percent of Germans, 29 percent of Greeks, and 38 percent of French think capitalism is the way to go.[17] You probably won't be surprised to learn that Europeans overwhelmingly supported Obama's reelection.[18]

So Europe has a mighty high opinion of the president. Europeans who used to grouse about crass American consumerism now admire Obama's statist economic policies. Just ask Industry Minister Arnaud Montebourg, a member of the governing Socialist party in France. As an advocate for nationalizing French steel companies, he told CNBC, "Barack Obama's nationalized. The Germans are nationalizing. All countries are nationalizing. I've also noticed the British nationalized six banks."[19]

So there.

But there are European countries and there are European countries. Poland and the Czech Republic are among the more pro-American nations in Europe—and it seems that almost as a consequence of that, Obama doesn't treat them as well as he treats Russia, which still regards us with suspicion if not enmity. On the one hand, Obama abandoned promises made by the United States to help build a missile defense system in Poland and the Czech Republic, in order to appease Russia. On the other hand, in order to appease Russia further, he was famously caught explaining to Dmitri Medvedev, then president of Russia, that he would have "more flexibility" dealing with missile defense issues once he won reelection.[20] In short, Obama's position on missile defense has been driven not by our commitments to our allies, but by what Russia wants, which is apparently what Obama wants.

What about our neighbors here in the Americas? Te queremos!

In April 2009, Obama published an op-ed that said, "Too often, the United States has not pursued and sustained engagement with our neighbors. We have been too easily distracted by other priorities, and have failed to see that our own progress is tied directly to progress throughout the Americas."[21] It's true. As you know, unlike nations like French Guiana or Belize, we're always so wrapped up in our own priorities. "The United States will be willing to acknowledge past errors where those errors have been made," Obama went on to say at the Summit of the Americas. "While the United States has done much to promote peace and prosperity in the hemisphere, we have at times been disengaged, and at times we sought to dictate our terms. But I pledge to you that we seek an equal partnership. There is no senior partner and junior partner in our relations; there is simply engagement based on mutual respect and common interests and shared values."[22] Does America really want to be an equal partner with Bolivia? Do we have mutual respect with Hugo Chavez of Venezuela? Do we have shared values with Communist Cuba? Not me.

The Future Must Not Belong to Those Who Slander the Prophet of Islam

But if anyone was truly deserving of our apologies, clearly it was the Muslim world.

Beyond the two famous speeches in Turkey and Cairo, there was much more. When NATO personnel inadvertently incinerated a few Korans (they were part of a larger cache of terrorist propaganda), Obama was quick with an apology. We all know that burning American flags and sacking embassies is what passes for group therapy in many parts of the Islamic world, so NATO officials, naturally, rushed to apologize, trying to avoid another outbreak of needless violence.[23]

President Obama, rather than, say, condemning the violence of Muslim mobs looking for an excuse to riot, or pointing out that NATO troops' accidental burning of Korans was as nothing compared to what NATO troops had done to liberate Afghanistan from the Taliban, instead wrote, according to the *New York Times*, to express his "deep regret for the reported incident. I extend to you and the Afghan people my sincere apologies."[24] Obama did not release the entire text of the letter so we're not sure what the rest entailed, but one can assume it was equally obsequious. Why the president of the United States should apologize to Hamid Karzai, the corrupt and ungrateful leader of Afghanistan, is something inquiring minds might like to know. Karzai and the Obama administration have had a tense relationship, so it seems likely that the apology was less personal than it was another instinctive bow to incendiary Islam. We inadvertently offend. They riot and burn American flags. We apologize. It's a regular pattern.

Obama might think he's allaying the anger of the Muslim street—though there is scant evidence of that, as that street erupts in riots regardless—but it also corrodes our own long-term standing in the world, which might be less impressed by our apologies than by our apparent weakness in the face of threats and riots. If the Muslim street thinks it is important to riot when a Koran is accidentally burned, do you think it respects a leader who does nothing when his own country's flag is burned in the street on purpose? Or do they take apologies for weakness?

Nor, one has to think, are they blind to Obama's repeated apologies to Islam and repeated refusals to condemn or intervene when Muslims attack Christians, which happens with alarming frequency in the Islamic world. In fact, at around the same time Obama was apologizing to Karzai, radical Muslims were using machetes to slaughter Christian farmers in Nigeria. Never heard about that? That's because Muslims killing Christians isn't news, especially when the White House doesn't think it is a major foreign policy concern of the United States.

In 2010, Libyan strongman Muammar Gaddafi took offense at Swiss voters approving, via referendum, a ban on the building of minarets. He called for a "jihad" against Switzerland. "Any Muslim in any part of the world who works with Switzerland is an apostate, is against Mohammad, God, and the Koran,"[25] Gaddafi said in a celebration in Benghazi to mark the Prophet's birthday. (That was probably news to many sheiks who did their banking business in Switzerland.) A State Department spokesman named P. J. Crowley sensibly commented that Gaddafi had "lots of words, not necessarily a lot of sense."[26] That's it. That's all he said. Crowley was forced to apologize by the Obama administration, explaining that his words did not reflect United States policy and were not intended to offend anyone—including, one presumes, jihadists and madmen.

It seems sometimes that every outburst of barbarism against the United States is met with a corresponding level of United States government contrition. Perhaps the most stunning example took place in 2012 on the anniversary of the September 11 terrorist attacks. A horde of Egyptian demonstrators scaled the walls of the U.S. Embassy in Cairo in a violent protest at a video they claimed insulted the Prophet Mohammed. The mob yanked down the American flag and replaced it with one that read, "There is no God but God, and Mohammad is his messenger."[27] The "movie," *Innocence of Muslims*, turned out to be a laughable, self-produced online travesty that no one in this country saw or even knew existed; it certainly had no link to the U.S. government. But the video was a useful pretext for rabble-rousers to whip excitable Islamists into violence that left more than 75 people dead in seven countries.

Now, if you yourself are an innocent, you might suppose that the United States stood resolutely behind the rights of free speech and free expression, and denied that any crackpot YouTube video was sufficient reason for violence against anyone. And of course you'd be wrong. Even before the attack, the American embassy in Cairo condemned "the continuing efforts by misguided individuals to hurt the religious feelings of Muslims—as we condemn efforts to offend believers of all religions. Today, the 11th anniversary of the September 11, 2001, terrorist attacks on the United States, Americans are honoring our patriots and those who serve our nation as the fitting response to the enemies of democracy. Respect for religious beliefs is a cornerstone of American democracy. We firmly reject the actions by those who abuse the universal right of free speech to hurt the religious beliefs of others."[28]

Is it possible that the Egyptian rabble has taken over the embassy and begun to issue press releases themselves? Had the embassy's communication department been outsourced to the Muslim Brotherhood? For a while onlookers were unsure. But no, it was simply an

Obama-era functionary using progressive rhetoric that had become pervasive in Washington. *Respect* for religious beliefs is not a cornerstone of American democracy; freedom of religion is. When the embassy's Obamaesque language stirred controversy stateside, the administration tried to distance itself from the press release (though no one, it seems, was ever fired or reprimanded for sending it out, perhaps because it was completely in line with the apologetic tone of the administration).

In public, and in the face of conservative criticism, the administration claimed it supported the First Amendment. Behind the scenes, the Obama administration tried to stifle free speech.[29] The administration, through White House spokesperson Jay Carney, conceded that it had "reached out to YouTube to call the video to their attention and ask them to review whether it violates their terms of use. We have made clear that we find it offensive and reprehensible and disgusting. We have denounced it. We have said we find it offensive and reprehensible, but we will not—you know, we cannot and will not squelch freedom of expression in this country."[30] Quick question, how many times do you think the Obama administration roused itself to denounce anti-Christian videos, widely available on YouTube, as "offensive and reprehensible"? If you said, "Never," guess what—you'd be right. And do any of us really think that when the federal government, wielding the full power of the regulatory state, asks a private business to "review" a matter, it isn't pressure, in this case against free speech? And let us be clear, there is nothing in the video that is obscene, pornographic, or graphically violent. The administration's opposition to the video is based solely on the fact that it is against the religion of Islam.

The video's repercussions didn't end there. Chairman of the Joint Chiefs of Staff, General Martin Dempsey, as a representative of the United States government, called on trailer-park pastor Terry Jones in Florida not to promote the film.[31] Pastor Jones is a kook whose fame is based entirely on the mainstream media's inability to ignore him; he's simply too attractive to television producers and newspaper scribblers. A few years earlier, Secretary of State Hillary Clinton rose to the bait and personally denounced him when he threatened to burn a Koran on the anniversary of the September 11 attacks. "It's regrettable that a pastor in Gainesville, Florida, with a church of no more than fifty people can make this outrageous and distressful, disgraceful plan and get, you know, the world's attention," said Clinton, who was getting the world's attention by pointing out what was happening.[32] The administration liked to make a big show of how it would denounce its own citizens in the name of tolerance.

Incidentally, Mark Basseley Youssef, the Coptic Christian and former gas station owner turned filmmaker who wrote and produced *The Innocence of Muslims*, was sentenced to a year in jail after he admitted to lying to his probation officer, using fake names, and violating the terms of his probation.[33] Federal investigators hopped on his trail after the video controversy. Youssef was also sentenced to death in absentia by our allies in Egypt for "insulting the Islamic religion through participating in producing and offering a movie that insults Islam and its prophet," said Judge Saif al-Nasr Soliman. As of this writing, no one was sentenced for trying to sack the American embassy.

Egypt wasn't alone.

Hundreds of protestors attacked security officials at the American embassy in Islamabad over the same movie.[34] In response, the Obama administration took out television advertisements featuring the president and Secretary of State Hillary Clinton condemning the video rather than defending the American Constitution (or condemning Islamist violence against American lives and property). Their words were subtitled in Urdu. "We absolutely reject its content and message," Clinton said, referring to the video.[35] Can one imagine the backlash if the administration had taken out ads apologizing to the Vatican for the airing of an anti-Catholic movie, such as *The Da Vinci Code*? Or if the administration had apologized to the Church of Jesus Christ of Latter-Day Saints for the anti-Mormon Broadway hit *The Book of Mormon*? Apologies are only reserved for those who threaten us with acts of violence.

At the same time as Egyptians and Pakistanis were expressing themselves by trying to burn down American embassies—and perhaps, if things went well, dragging a few American bodies across the streets—a heavily armed group attacked the U.S. diplomatic mission in Benghazi, killing U.S. Ambassador J. Christopher Stevens and three other Americans. For weeks afterwards the president and his administration insisted that this was no premeditated act of terrorism but just another riot over the YouTube video. If it had been an act of terrorism, it would have been an embarrassment to an administration that claimed that terrorism was receding and that prided itself on improving relations with the Islamic world. Luckily, the media went with the Obama version about the YouTube video and accepted the administration spin that the real story was Mitt Romney's unseemly "political" criticisms of the administration's response to the attack.

Two weeks later, when President Obama spoke before the United Nations General Assembly, he again condemned the anti-Islam video and apologized for it. Then he said something truly remarkable for an American president:

> That is what we saw play out the last two weeks, as a crude and disgusting video sparked outrage throughout the Muslim world. I have made it clear that the United States

government had nothing to do with this video, and I believe its message must be rejected by all who respect our common humanity. It is an insult not only to Muslims, but to America as well—for as the city outside these walls makes clear, we are a country that has welcomed people of every race and religion. We are home to Muslims who worship across our country. We not only respect the freedom of religion—we have laws that protect individuals from being harmed because of how they look or what they believe....

The future must not belong to those who slander the prophet of Islam.[36]

Since when has the president of the United States been named mullah in chief? When did defending Islam become part of his job description? And when did it become the proper role of an American president to apologize for tacky videos on YouTube? (That could be a full-time job if he wants it.) And when did it become the job of the president to deny the right of critics of any religion (or ideology) to mock or satirize beliefs with which they disagree? Had Obama been president in 1807, and been as solicitous for Christians as he is for Muslims, would he have condemned Tom Paine for writing *The Age of Reason* and apologized to Christians around the world for any offense Paine had caused?

Obama swore to defend the Constitution, not the sensitivities of foreigners. Yet one of the first actions of the administration was to rejoin the absurdly named United Nations Human Rights Council—which has had an array of interesting members, including China, Qatar, Angola, Cuba, Syria, Saudi Arabia, Russia, and even some states where slavery still exists, like Mauritania. In 2010, Muammar Gaddafi's Libya won a seat on the council with a 155-vote margin. President

George W. Bush rightly had boycotted the human rights commission as a fraud. The Obama administration thought otherwise and had ambassador Susan Rice leading the administration's efforts for "a new era of engagement" at the United Nations. What did this engagement achieve? As a member of the Human Rights Council, the United States co-sponsored a resolution that advocated restricting free speech in the name of political correctness. According to the resolution, the "exercise of the right to freedom of expression carries with it special duties and responsibilities" and any "negative racial and religious stereotyping" should be condemned. The media, states the resolution, has a "social responsibility" to develop "voluntary codes of professional ethical conduct" that will adhere to the sensitivities of the United Nations and its gaggle of authoritarian governments.[37] You can bet that while the Prophet Mohammad might be protected, they won't be so sensitive to the feelings of Jews or Christians. But that's almost beside the point. It is simply anti-American (in the purest sense of the word) to join any action that calls for the inhibition of political and religious speech. In a free society, criticizing Islam should be fair game. In a free society, we should be able to say and think what we like. In a free society…but is that what we're losing, as political correctness and foreign policy appeasement displace the First Amendment? In our foreign policy we seem to have an identity crisis: under Obama, we no longer know who we are and what we stand for as Americans. Instead, we make excuses for mobs that attack our embassies and agree with autocracies that want to curtail our freedoms.

The New World

In September 2012, the Obama administration notified Congress that it would provide Egypt's new government an emergency cash infusion of around $450 million[38]—or in other words, the radical Muslim Brotherhood running Egypt were getting a bit of pocket change to go along with the $2 billion allowance they already receive from us. Remember that around $1.3 billion of this funding is marked for military spending, since aid for infrastructure or economic growth is a secondary concern to Egyptian regimes. What they desire is a world-class military force, because you never know when Eritrea is going to get aggressive. The new aid was part of around $1 billion in supplementary assistance that, as the *New York Times* put it, "the Obama administration has pledged to Egypt to bolster its transition to democracy after the overthrow last year of the former president, Hosni Mubarak."

How is that transition to democracy working out?

After receiving the extra funding, Egypt's president Mohammed Morsi did what nearly every "president" in the Muslim world does after attaining power: he attempted to become an autocrat. Morsi granted himself immunity from the courts and extended the same protection to his Islamist allies so they could draft a new constitution without the judicial system hampering progress. He then decreed that every pronouncement he's made since gaining power would also be immune from judicial oversight. To put this in perspective, remember that in his famous Cairo speech Obama said that for "over a thousand years, Al-Azhar [an Islamic university of Sunni dogma] has stood as a beacon of Islamic learning, and for over a century, Cairo University has been a source of Egypt's advancement. Together, you represent the harmony between tradition and progress." Now, with the president's blessing, Al-Azhar's Islamic leadership was crafting Egypt's constitution to comport with Sharia law. Progress and harmony is measured in Egypt and elsewhere in the Arab world, especially after the Arab Spring, not as we would measure it but as "progress" away from Western norms to Sharia law. There is not much liberty in Sharia law, and not much tolerance either. If you want misogynistic, anti-Christian, anti-Jewish laws and the sort of legal regime preferred by the Taliban and Osama bin Laden, then Sharia is your thing. It is not clear why it should be ours.

Appeasement of Islamic radicalism is one thing; helping bolster it is another. Under Obama, we're doing both. Many Americans had high hopes for the Arab Spring revolution, because we instinctively think of revolutions against autocrats as inherently good and assume the rebels share our democratic ideals. While some might, most in the Arab world do not. Islamist regimes are popular. In the Gaza strip, right next to Egypt, sits Hamas, a terrorist political party and popularly elected government. Any hope of progress in Egypt quickly dissipated when the Muslim Brotherhood decisively won national elections. Rather than apply pressure to foster moderation, President Obama backed the Islamic government's ascendency to power.

Even after riots broke out and Egypt's presidential palace was surrounded by citizens protesting the deterioration of their short-lived liberty, President Obama called on President Morsi "to build on a growing rapport with his Egyptian counterpart" and to counsel Morsi "that it was in his own interest to offer his opposition compromises, in order to build trust in his government"[39]—this according to the *New York Times* citing "a senior Obama administration official." The story was written by *New York Times* Cairo bureau chief David K. Kirkpatrick, who described the Muslim Brotherhood as a "moderate, regular old political force."[40] The mainstream media, and the Obama administration, seemed content to ignore that Egypt was being transformed into an Islamist state.

In an interview with the Spanish-language network Telemundo, given less than 24 hours after a violent mob stormed our embassy in

Cairo, Obama said the Muslim Brotherhood government was still trying to find its way. "They were democratically elected. I think we are going to have to see how they respond to this incident, to see how they respond to maintaining the peace treaty with Israel." He also said that while Egypt wasn't an ally, it wasn't an enemy either. The State Department quickly corrected the president by explaining that Egypt was, in fact, a major non-NATO ally—a designation the country was awarded in 1989,[41] though maybe that designation should be revisited, because if Egypt isn't an ally, why do we give them $2 billion a year—does that seem like a wise investment? Egypt might be more democratic, at least temporarily, than it was under Mubarak, but is it actually freer? More important from our perspective, is it more or less inclined to remain at peace with Israel? Is it more or less inclined to be a voice of moderation in the Arab world? Is it more or less likely to harbor Islamist terrorists?

And since we're asking questions, maybe we should ask this one: does it matter that Egypt has a democratic government, if that government is a government hostile to the United States, our interests, and our values? Democracy means elections, but what really counts is the culture of the people who are voting. In his superb book, *The Servile Mind: How Democracy Erodes the Moral Life*, Kenneth Minogue argues that the history of both "traditional societies and totalitarian states of the twentieth century suggested that many people are, in most circumstances, happy to sink themselves in some collective enterprise that guides their lives and guarantees them security." It is a myth that people always yearn for freedom. Humans aren't hard-wired for freedom. Americans are. Or, at least, we were. But a great many other people prefer security to freedom, or prefer to be part of a great totalitarian cause, as long as they get to wear a Che t-shirt and believe they're fighting for "the people," or would like to establish a new caliphate for Islam to rule every aspect of our lives.

Freedom means different things to different people. The movement that ousted Mubarak did so in the name of freedom. But what do Egyptians actually believe? According to a recent Pew poll, 54 percent of Egyptians believe that women and men should be segregated in the workplace; 82 percent believe that adulterers should be stoned; 84 percent believe that apostates of Islam should face the death penalty; and 77 percent believe thieves should be flogged or have their hands cut off. And 99 percent of Americans—just a guess—wouldn't want to live under that kind of democracy, even if it meant a popular national vote for president.

Now, admittedly, it was George W. Bush who argued that humanity was innately wired for freedom. No doubt, this notion makes sense to the average American. That's why we sent so many young men and women to die for the freedom of others and why we continue to stick our noses into every corner of the globe. Americans tend to be evangelical about the ideas of freedom and democracy. On the other hand, Obama struck a chord when he said, "No system of government can or should be imposed by one nation by any other," clearly referring to Bush-era nation-building. While Americans think democracy is great and everyone should have it, and have done more than their share to fight to defend it and erect it around the world, Americans loathe the idea of empire-building. America might have global interests, but talk to any American and you'll quickly see that the idea of global empire is anathema.

The question is how to defend those interests. George W. Bush pushed for democracy in the Arab world, but he also cared about the outcome, prodding Arab leaders towards freedom. President Obama, however, seems perfectly content with elected Islamists in power.

Bush believed, at bottom, whether he understood this or not, in a democracy grounded in a Judeo-Christian moral foundation, not a democracy electing governments to impose Sharia law. He believed in democracy that brought with it economic freedom and respect for individual rights. Obama is not so judgmental, at least in this regard. Almost like a cartoon version of a radical liberal, Obama is equally at ease supporting Muslim governments, ignoring Muslim persecution of Christians, and putting the United States behind lobbying efforts for homosexual rights abroad.[42] Similarly, he can be simultaneously a passionate opponent of the war in Iraq as well as the "drone attack" president, the president who wound down our war in Afghanistan while getting us involved in the overthrow of Muammar Gaddafi in Libya. At least George W. Bush fought his wars with congressional approval, as per the Constitution, and did so with relatively open aims, even though they got muddied as nation-building took over from the original missions of toppling the Taliban which sheltered bin Laden and toppling Saddam Hussein while neutralizing his presumed weapons of mass destruction. When Obama joined the NATO bombing campaign that dislodged Gaddafi, he did not seek congressional approval, which the War Powers Act of 1973 explicitly required—setting, in the words of Yale's law and political science professor Bruce Ackerman, "a troubling precedent that could allow future administrations to wage war at their convenience, free of legislative checks and balances."[43]

Beyond that, what was the American objective in Libya? That was never exactly clear. Even less clear was the identity of our Libyan allies on the ground. During the half-year campaign by rebels to drive Muammar Gaddafi from power, the administration consistently downplayed any possibility that we were actually assisting Islamist forces in Libya. As soon as Gaddafi was toppled, however, we learned

that the CIA was, from the start, worried about Islamist radicals seiz-
ing power. Bruce Riedel, a former senior CIA analyst who has advised
President Obama, told Reuters, for instance, that there was widespread concern that Islamists would make Libya a base for Islamic
militants, spreading trouble from Algeria to the Sinai Peninsula. "It's
of concern that terrorists are going to take advantage of instability,"
said one U.S. official. "There is a potential problem," said another U.S.
official.[44] There sure was. After Gaddafi was gone, it became apparent
that prominent leaders of the Libyan rebels were Islamists and that
Islamists would be part of the new Libyan regime. Mahmoud Jibril,
the former interim prime minister, was open about this, saying, "In
a national dialogue, no one is excluded: no Salafis, no al-Qaeda, no
Ansar al-Sharia will be excluded."[45] Well, that's comforting.

Consequences of Moral Equivalence

Obama, apparently, has little problem supporting Islamists in
Egypt and elsewhere. But when it comes to oppressed Muslims rising
against a tyrannical regime that considers America the great Satan
and that seems to be fast-tracking its way to a nuclear bomb—well,
he's not sure so sure about that. After the sham reelection of Iranian
President Mahmoud Ahmadinejad in 2009, the Iranian Green Movement took to the streets against that totalitarian regime. Yet it was not
until 2011, two years after it really mattered, that Obama even mentioned the uprising. Why? Well, it's one thing for Obama to support
revolutions against an American ally in Egypt and a tamed former
terrorist-supporter in Libya. It's another to have the audacity to actually support action against an open enemy of the United States. That's
the famous way of liberal American foreign policy. If you're an American ally—think Jimmy Carter and the Shah of Iran—you're screwed.

If you're an American enemy, appeasement is the order of the day. When he could have supported it, Obama let the Green revolution die on the vine.

Many believe that Iran will soon have nuclear weapons. If the Iranian regime achieves this breakthrough, it will have been done in defiance of international law, United Nations resolutions, the International Atomic Energy Agency, and just about everything else in which Barack Obama told us to put our trust. A nuclear-armed Iran could threaten not just Israel, but Saudi Arabia and every other Sunni government in the Arab world. If anyone wanted to destabilize the Middle East, this would do the trick. And Obama, with his great faith in diplomacy, and in the innate superiority of his conciliatory approach to George W. Bush's strident pro-Americanism, has achieved what exactly to prevent this? The official United States government National Intelligence Estimate reports that Iran is much closer to developing a nuclear weapon. According to the Israeli newspaper *Haaretz*, "The NIE contends that Iran has made surprising, notable progress in the research and development of key components of its military nuclear program."[46] In another report, defense experts maintained that Iran's Fordow nuclear site was hidden so deep underground that it was safe from conventional air strikes, and that if Israel hoped to stop Iran's nuclear program by force, it would have to attack the site with special ground forces or with ballistic missiles armed with tactical nuclear warheads.[47] In October 2012, the Institute for Science and International Security released a report concluding that by early 2013, Iran will be able to produce enough highly enriched uranium for at least one atomic bomb at its Nantaz facility.[48] In November 2012, the International Atomic Energy Agency reported that Iran installed 700 new centrifuges at its fortified underground facility at Fordow—the facility is now believed to house approximately

2,800 centrifuges. The IAEA believes Iran could develop a nuclear warhead within months.[49]

One would think that these reports, and others that land on his desk, would sufficiently alarm President Obama for him to take some sort of action. But Obama has stayed the course with economic sanctions and negotiations. It is not certain, however, that sanctions have any useful effect at all—hurting individuals rather than governments—but even if they do, the Obama administration likes to take credit for policies it has opposed. Not only have sanctions of various sorts been in place against Iran for decades, but also Obama actually tried to water down an amendment to the National Defense Authorization Act in 2010 that made them tougher. (He eventually signed the Comprehensive Iran Sanctions, Accountability, and Divestment Act of 2010 after both houses of Congress passed it overwhelmingly.) Then, in 2012, Democrat Robert Menendez and Republican Mark Kirk introduced an amendment to the National Defense Authorization Act (which passed 94 to 0) that proposed still tighter sanctions on Iran. According to *Foreign Policy* magazine, "The legislation would also vastly expand U.S. support for human rights inside Iran and impose new sanctions on Iranians who divert humanitarian assistance from its intended purpose." The president opposed the legislation. National Security Spokesman Tommy Vietor told *Foreign Policy*, "As we focus with our partners on effectively implementing these efforts, we believe additional authorities now threaten to undercut these efforts."[50]

Friend or Foe?

In late 2012, Khaled Meshal, leader of Hamas in Gaza, thanked Egypt and Iran for their support of Hamas's eight-day-long rocket barrage against Israeli citizens—that would be Egypt our "ally," with its democratic Muslim Brotherhood government, and Iran, whose domestic opposition movement President Obama refused to support. The United States used to be unmistakably in favor of Israel because Israel shared our western values. President Obama thinks a more nuanced, balanced approach is called for—one that, in fact, sees Israel as the intransigent bully standing in the way of Middle Eastern peace.

The conservative scholar George Gilder argued in his book *The Israel Test* that where you stand on the Jewish State—not always, not in every policy area, but in general—is a relatively strong indication about how you feel about the deeper ideals of liberty and capitalism. The debate over Israel, he asserts, is the manifestation of a deeper moral and ideological war around the world. "The real issue," writes Gilder, "is between the rule of law and the rule of leveler egalitarianism, between creative excellence and covetous 'fairness,' between admiration of achievement versus envy and resentment of it."

If you accept this formulation as I do, then Obama's agenda towards Israel makes all the sense in the world. Never has there been a president so antagonistic towards Israel. Never has one been so intent on isolating the Jewish State. During the 2012 election season, the administration did its best to temper many of its anti-Israel positions, because they were offending Jewish donors to the Democratic Party and because the administration knows its Middle Eastern policy is unpopular. A 2011 Gallup poll, for instance, found that 80 percent of Republicans, 71 percent of independents, and 65 percent of Democrats have a favorable view of Israel; only 19 percent have a similar view of Palestinians.[51] But now that Obama is safely reelected, we can expect a much more pro-Palestinian administration.

In his first term, Obama never found time to visit Israel, though he visited Egypt (less than an hour away by plane), Saudi Arabia (same), Turkey, and Iraq, each time unfurling his agenda of appeasing militant Islam. Obama is a leftist, and, as such, sees Israel as the colonial aggressor in the Middle East.

When running for president in 2008, Obama claimed, "There is a strain within the pro-Israel community that says unless you adopt an unwavering pro-Likud approach to Israel that you're anti-Israel."[52] Likud is the major right-of-center party in Israel, and, as I write, the elected party of power. Obama is definitely not on their side. But it's not clear that he's on any Israeli side that is not in favor of retreat and surrender.

Obama avoids disparaging any "democratically" elected leaders in the Arab world, but he had no problem belittling a pro-American party in Israel before speaking to its leader (who in fact was to become the next prime minister of Israel). Perhaps this is because Obama believes America is far too close to Israel; we need some critical distance. When Malcolm Hoenlein, the executive vice chairman of the Conference of Presidents of Major American Jewish Organizations, told the president, "If you want Israel to take risks, then its leaders must know that the United States is right next to them," Obama replied, "Look at the past eight years. During those eight years, there was no space between Israel and us, and what did we get from that? When there is no daylight, Israel just sits on the sidelines, and that erodes our credibility with the Arab states."[53]

What do we get from being close to Israel? It depends on the ideological prism you view the world through, I suppose. If your goal is to gain credibility with autocratic Arab States, if you want to placate Arab tyrants and allow them to dictate the contours of the future Middle East, then maybe it makes sense to step away from Israel. (But do we really gain credibility with our enemies when we abandon our allies?) If, on the other hand, you believe that our foreign policy should be guided by efforts to strengthen our bonds with countries that share our moral and ideological values, then being close to Israel makes perfect sense.

Some defenders of the president contend that Obama's hostility towards Israel is simply part of his broader antagonism towards the Likud government and a personal rift with its leader, Prime Minister Benjamin Netanyahu. After all, this is the same President Obama who told French President Nicolas Sarkozy that he loathed having to deal with Netanyahu.[54] He has certainly never bowed to him, as he did to Saudi Arabia's King Abdullah, or assured us that we need to respect the Likud government because it was democratically elected (like the Islamic brotherhood in Egypt). His dislike for Netanyahu seems palpable, but so does his dislike for what he sees as an aggressive, pro-Western Israel that is at odds with his foreign policy of appeasing militant Islam.

Obama denied a request from Netanyahu for a meeting in September 2012, when both leaders attended a United Nations conference. Even the left-leaning news service Reuters called this an "unusual snub."[55] While the president found time to make another appearance on the *Late Show* with David Letterman, he could not meet with America's foremost ally in the Middle East to discuss the growing threat of Iran's nuclear program.[56] A lesser noticed but almost equally telling snub was that President Obama's United Nations ambassador, Susan Rice, didn't even attend the Israeli prime minister's speech to the United Nations General Assembly when he laid out the Iranian nuclear threat.[57] Ultimately, the president did agree to a phone meeting with the prime minister, though he soon after referred to Netanyahu's warnings about Iran as "noise" that he "blocks out."[58]

In 2010, the White House became so agitated with a new Israeli housing project, announced while Vice President Joe Biden was visiting Israel, that the casual onlooker might have thought that the Jerusalem neighborhood in question was the one sticking point to achieving a Palestinian-Israeli peace. The housing development was, in fact, merely an expansion of an already established Israeli settlement. While the Obama administration might not like the idea of Israeli expansion, building 1,500 new homes in northern Jerusalem was hardly an act of war or terrorism. Yet, according to *The Jerusalem Post*, Hillary Clinton telephoned Netanyahu—who, along with many other Israeli officials, apologized for the poor timing of the project's announcement—to "berate," "rebuke," "warn," and "condemn" Israel.[59] White House senior adviser David Axelrod used NBC's *Meet the Press* to call the incident an "affront," an "insult," and "very, very destructive."[60] While the administration chastised Israel, the Palestinian Authority was meanwhile preparing to dedicate Dalal Mughrabi Square. You know, just a place for folks to gather and commemorate the 32nd anniversary of 1978's Coastal Road Massacre, in which 37 Israelis—13 of them children—were murdered in a bus hijacking. An American named Gail Rubin, who happened to be snapping some nature pictures in the area, was also gunned down.

No worries. No affront taken. That's not "very, very destructive" to the peace process in the Middle East. Obama was above the fray, above frivolous notions of "allies" or "friends." No worries about a monument to a mass killing whose victims included an American. After all, it was an important moment in Palestinian liberation history. We don't want to upset the fragile mood of the Arab street.

If the purpose of this double standard is to show American support for handing over parts of Jerusalem to the corrupt Palestinian government of Fatah, well, I suppose that's in accord with Obama's foreign policy of appeasing our enemies and spiting our allies. If the purpose is to push for a Jewish-free West Bank to create goodwill with the Muslim world, good luck with that. Not many international agreements feature ethnic cleansing clauses. But everyone knows that—unlike the millions of Arabs who live within Israel proper—if any Jews are left on a West Bank that is given to Fatah, they will be slaughtered, bombed from their homes, and rocketed from their schools. It is odd indeed that an American president should take the position that it is wise and just to retract Israel's borders, and appease the ethnic-cleansers.

But that does seem to be Obama's position. In May 2011, he suggested that Israel use its 1967 borders as a starting point for any negotiations[61] with the Arabs—knowing full well that Israel considers those borders to be indefensible for very sound reasons. Obama, speaking in front of the United Nations General Assembly, also insisted that Israel and the Palestinians negotiate "without preconditions." This tact, Obama hoped, would lead to "two states living side by side in peace and security—a Jewish state of Israel with true security for all Israelis and a viable, independent Palestinian state with contiguous territory that ends the occupation that began in 1967 and realizes the potential of the Palestinian people." If Obama expects Israel to engage in negotiations without preconditions, then he expects Israel to negotiate with terrorists, which is something the United States won't do, at any rate not officially. But perhaps that is changing under Obama. Obama expects Israel to end the "occupation" of the West Bank that began in 1967; he also expects Israel to abandon sections of its capital city, Jerusalem. During his trip to Israel Republican presidential candidate Mitt Romney commented, "it is a deeply moving experience to be in Jerusalem, the capital of Israel." Somehow this declaration of a fact was transformed into a "gaffe" by the media, because recognizing Israel's capital is considered controversial. Needless to say, the Obama administration took a shot at

Romney's foreign policy "fumble." And in response to the candidate's innocuous declaration, White House Deputy Press Secretary Josh Earnest stated: "Well, our view is that that's a different position than this administration holds. It's the view of this administration that the capital is something that should be determined in final status negotiations between the parties."[62]

Funny, because when addressing the American Israel Public Affairs Committee on June 4, 2008, as a Democratic presidential hopeful, Barack Obama said, "Jerusalem will remain the capital of Israel, and it must remain undivided."[63] Like Romney, Obama upset the perpetually upset Palestinian government. Naturally, Obama immediately backtracked, saying, "Well, obviously, it's going to be up to the parties to negotiate a range of these issues. And Jerusalem will be part of those negotiations."[64] On the question of Jerusalem, Romney was in the company of other noted Likudnick radicals like Bill Clinton, who, during the 1992 campaign, said that he would "recognize Jerusalem as an undivided city, the eternal capital of Israel, and I believe in the principle of moving our embassy to Jerusalem," and John Kerry, whose campaign material in 2004 stated that he "has long advocated moving the U.S. Embassy to Jerusalem, Israel's indisputable capital. In 1999, he signed a letter taking President Clinton to task for not moving the embassy."

Then there is, naturally, the more central question of cultural values. On a campaign visit to Jerusalem in 2012, Romney put forth this notion: "Culture makes all the difference. And as I come here and I look out over this city and consider the accomplishments of the people of this nation, I recognize the power of at least culture and a few other things." It was immediately treated as some sort of contentious declaration.[65] Colin Kahl, an Obama campaign foreign policy advisor who worked at the Pentagon, claimed that if someone like

Romney were in charge, Americans would abdicate any chance of being "seen as an honest broker."[66] These were, he went on, "extraordinarily complicated and delicate issues and is not something you can just wing it on and expect not to make some mistakes, and Governor Romney made a big one."

Obama had been so critical of Israel that in 2010, seventy-six U.S. Senators—including thirty-eight Democrats—did something quite unusual and crafted a letter asking the administration to tone it down.[67]

> We also urge you to reaffirm the unbreakable bonds that tie the United States and Israel together and to diligently work to defuse current tensions. The Israeli and U.S. governments will undoubtedly, at times, disagree over policy decisions. But disagreements should not adversely affect our mutual interests—including restarting the peace process between Israel and her neighbors and preventing Iran from acquiring nuclear weapons.

Not long after, Netanyahu spoke in front of a joint session of Congress and received 29 standing ovations.[68] The real shame was that the Israeli prime minister had to remind us why the United States and Israel enjoy a close relationship, something we've lost track of during the Obama administration. It's because, in a world still rife with tyranny and oppression, we're not like everyone else.

Except to Obama, we are.

CHAPTER FIVE

THE MORTAL CLIFF

*"And then your Mommy said, 'Just do it, already!' which was very
confusing to Daddy, so I took the most literal translation... [quietly]
but between you and me, it was the smartest thing
I ever did, 'cause now you're here."*
—BEN STONE, *KNOCKED UP*

*"Democracy demands that the religiously motivated translate their
concerns into universal, rather than religion-specific, values.
It requires that their proposals be subject to argument, and amenable
to reason. I may be opposed to abortion for religious reasons, but if I
seek to pass a law banning the practice, I cannot simply point to the
teachings of my church or evoke God's will.... Now this is going to be
difficult for some who believe in the inerrancy of the Bible, as many
evangelicals do. But in a pluralistic democracy, we have no choice.
Politics depends on our ability to persuade each other of common
aims based on a common reality. It involves the compromise,
the art of what's possible. At some fundamental level, religion does
not allow for compromise. It's the art of the impossible."*
—BARACK OBAMA, SOJOURNERS/CALL TO RENEWAL ADDRESS
ON FAITH AND POLITICS, JUNE 26, 2006

Life as We Knew It

When it comes to abortion, Barack Obama is not "amenable to reason."

The purpose of this chapter isn't to rehash the traditional argument over abortion—though it is certainly a worthwhile conversation to have—but rather to argue that Obama's presidency has changed that debate forever. Obama and his allies have waged a crusade to make abortion mainstream, to strip it of consequences, to inject it with relativism, and to ensure that it becomes a fundamental American right, offered and paid for by every one of us—even those of us with religious or conscience objections—through government coercion.

Barack Obama, the same president who fought relentlessly to pass legislation that compelled us all to partake in government-controlled health care, the man who berated the Supreme Court for its Citizens United decision that defended free speech, the same president who consistently offers policy prescriptions that place new limitations on liberty in the name of fairness, believes that abortion, which by any scientific or moral measurement ends a human life, "is one of the most fundamental rights we possess."[1]

It was Nat Hentoff, the civil libertarian, noted jazz critic, and longtime columnist for the *Village Voice*, who noted that as a reporter he could usually "understand why people with whom I disagree think and act the way they do," but, he went on, "I am at a loss to understand how an abortionist finds his daily vocation in deliberately, brutally ending a human life."[2] I don't either. Like many who share my upbringing as a secular, urban Northerner, I was once pro-choice. The idea that abortion was a woman's right to decide her destiny and none of my damn business was pounded into my consciousness through TV, movies, books, and government-provided education from my childhood. Admittedly, it was also a rather convenient position for someone who grew up embracing libertarian positions. The notions of "choice" and "freedom" are enticing to a lot of people—even if what qualifies as "choice" and "freedom" can get distorted or given a very incomplete view. It's certainly easy to entice irresponsible young people with options. The idea of abortion as a "choice"—a fallback option if you can't prevent a pregnancy in some other way—is sure to appeal to a lot of young men and women, who desire the freedom to engage in sexual activity but don't want the responsibility of a child. It all seems like sensible self-interest—until a person is honest enough to follow the logical and moral consequences of abortion to their ugly conclusions.

It is fair to say that abortion is a personal topic—often a personal tragedy. My own transformation—I prefer to think of it as an evolution, if I may borrow a phrase from the Obama lexicon—to a pro-life position began with the birth of my first child, and it further solidified with the birth of my second. A new baby (and one of mine was born prematurely) transforms any theoretical argument about life's beginnings and makes them very real, very quickly. But it was more than that. It is science and reason that offer the most compelling argument for life.

A few years back, while I was a columnist at the *Denver Post*, a hit-and-run driver struck a pregnant woman in my exceptionally liberal neighborhood. Tragically, the women lost her child. The incident was met with widespread alarm. Throughout my neighborhood, there was an outpouring of support and sadness. These were good people here. Flowers, teddy bears, and condolence notes were left at the corner where the incident occurred. Conversations moved from what a horrible tragedy it was to whether the assailant (never caught, to my knowledge) should be charged with manslaughter or murder?

Had that fetus been a few weeks younger a doctor could have performed a surgical procedure on it and terminated its life, and there would be no grieving, no one leaving signs for the dead, and no talk of murder. The fact is that if the mother had displayed sufficient mental anguish, real or imagined, she could have taken the drive up to Boulder, only an hour north of Denver, that very day, and visited a "Doctor" Warren Hern, a professional late-term abortionist, who would have changed that "baby" into a "fetus"—a linguistic substitution with profound consequences for at least one human being—and put an end to the entire arrangement. "The sensations of dismemberment flow through the forceps like an electric current," said Hern at one American Association of Planned Parenthood Physicians meeting.[3]

Does life really begin on the say-so of a single person—even the mother? Does her position or mental state change what a fetus is or is not? That kind of elastic calculation grinds against reason and yet it is the underlying logic of the liberal argument on abortion. As Congressman Ron Paul of Texas, who is an ob-gyn, once explained, "people ask an expectant mother how her baby is doing. They do not ask how her fetus is doing, or her blob of tissue, or her parasite."[4] Abortion supporters have a hard time winning a logical argument, which is why they lard up the issue of abortion with layers of cultural and political baggage.

Science and medical progress are changing minds. A full-term pregnancy lasts about 40 weeks. Premature babies can survive if born after about 22 to 24 weeks. What happens when we can keep a baby alive at 20 weeks or 15 weeks? We are already at the stage where babies are aborted at an age where they could be kept alive. And when does a baby feel pain? Studies have yet to come to a definitive answer on this question (and I'm not sure it should matter in defining when life starts), but signs point to it being far earlier than previously thought.

Sonograms, naturally, have also given us an incredibly detailed look at little human beings. Many states have attempted to enact laws that mandate that abortion providers show ultrasounds to prospective customers. Though I oppose these efforts on First Amendment grounds, the arguments liberals offer against them are extraordinarily telling. The pro-choice Guttmacher Institute, for instance, recently released a "State Policies in Brief," concerning "Requirements for Ultrasound" that laid it out as so: "Since routine ultrasound is not considered medically necessary as a component of first-trimester abortion, the requirements appear to be a veiled attempt to personify the fetus and dissuade a woman from obtaining an abortion."[5]

Is an abortion "medically necessary"? Personifying a human being, even a nascent human being, isn't really that difficult considering we're talking about a person. But the argument against personifying also tells us that abortionists understand the moral implications of fully comprehending that we're terminating a life, and they understand that young women and secular Americans might have their minds changed. That pro-choice advocates find the truth troubling—and want to hide it—is itself troubling. As Christopher Hitchens, that late provocateur and devoted atheist wrote in—believe it or not—his book *God Is Not Great*:

> As a materialist, I think it has been demonstrated that an embryo is a separate body and entity, and not merely (as some really did used to argue) a growth on or in the female body. There used to be feminists who would say that it was more like an appendix or even—this was seriously maintained—a tumor. That nonsense seems to have stopped. Of the considerations that have stopped it, one is the fascinating and moving view provided by the sonogram, and

another is the survival of "premature" babies of feather-like weight, who have achieved "viability" outside the womb.... The words "unborn child," even when used in a politicized manner, describe a material reality.[6]

Despite media depictions of pro-lifers as a bunch of religious nuts, the contours of the argument have long favored pro-life advocates. Democrats, at least in the past, conceded that abortion was perhaps something a little unsavory. The Democratic mantra was that abortion should be safe, legal, *and rare*. They implied that abortion was not a moral good in itself; it was rather something society should work to reduce, usually by ramping up spending on sex education and family planning clinics. Only the Catholic Church, to my knowledge, took the provocative position that contraception and abortion aren't either-ors but both-ands—that is, one inevitably leads to the other by separating sex from reproduction. Catholic Democrats generally ignored the contraception part of their Church's teaching, and squared the circle on abortion by saying that while they were personally opposed to abortion, they would not let their religious beliefs interfere with keeping abortion legal. The rhetorical idea was still to keep a little distance from abortion itself.

No more. Obama-era progressives have changed all that. Abortion is now framed as a victory over regressive hillbillies and evil, ignorant Republican men; a victory for women from the bonds of motherhood that would take them back to the 1950s; a victory for the young whose careers or freedoms might be derailed by the arrival of a child (Obama himself said, on the campaign trail in 2008, that he didn't want his daughters "punished with a baby" that might arrive at an inconvenient moment).[7] Abortion is no longer an ugly choice, but simply a choice that in many cases makes perfect sense. The left has politicized abortion. It is not simply, as the pro-lifers see it, an issue about a fundamental right to life; it is wrapped up in broader social and economic battles about equality, women's health, and social progress.

Despite the Democratic Party's hyper-politicization of abortion—and despite the tragedy of more than a million dead every year—abortion rates are going down or have at least stabilized.

From 1973 through 2008, nearly 50 million legal abortions have occurred in the United States,[8] a disaster on countless levels. The annual number of legal abortions in the United States doubled between 1973—the year *Roe v. Wade* struck down state prohibitions on aborting babies, declaring it a constitutional right—and 1979. Abortion rates peaked in 1990. A study from the pro-choice Guttmacher Institute found that in that year there were 1.6 million performed and the abortion rate was 27.4 per 1,000 women.[9] Between 2000 and 2009, the number of annual abortions decreased by 6 percent. In 2008, approximately 1.21 million abortions were performed in the United States, down from 1.29 million in 2002, 1.31 million in 2000, and 1.36 million in 1996.[10]

Our attitude about abortion, not surprisingly, mirrored these numbers. In May 2009, Gallup's annual Values and Beliefs survey found that for the first time since it began polling decades earlier, more Americans identified themselves as pro-life than pro-choice. This represented a significant shift from earlier in the decade when 50 percent of Americans were pro-choice and 44 percent were pro-life. Those polled were given three options that identified the extent to which they believed abortion should be legal. Roughly the same amount of Americans said that procedure should be illegal in all circumstances (23 percent) as said it should be legal under any circumstances (22 percent). Asked to pick one of the two labels applied to the abortion debate, a full 50 percent said they were pro-life, whereas only 41 percent said they were pro-choice, down from the previous low of 42 percent.[11]

Now? It appears that the left's strategy of politicizing abortion is working. In the summer of 2012, when Obama was in full campaign mode and the Democrats were railing against an alleged Republican "war on women," a Pew poll found that 54 percent of Americans supported legal abortion "in all or most cases." Only 42 percent said that abortion should be illegal in most or all cases.[12] (In similar polling in 2009, 46 percent favored and 44 percent opposed abortion in most or all cases.) In 2012, nearly two-thirds of Democrats said that abortion should be legal "in all or most cases"—and, more alarmingly, so did 58 percent of independents. Even a slim majority of Catholics (52 percent) supported abortion in all or most cases.

A November 2012 Rasmussen Reports poll had even worse news for pro-lifers. Among likely voters, 54 percent described themselves as pro-choice on the issue of abortion, while 38 percent said they were pro-life.[13] Two other polls that were conducted around the same time showed a similar trend toward increasing support for abortion. It is hard to see how this change is for the better.

Whenever, and for Whatever Reason

The president says that "abortion is a moral issue," that "it's one that families struggle with all the time," and "that in wrestling with those issues, I don't think that the government criminalizing the choices that families make is the best answer for reducing abortions."[14] But does the president want to reduce abortions?

In 2007, Obama told Planned Parenthood Action Fund that his *first act* in the White House would be to sign the Freedom of Choice Act—a bill that would codify the right to abortion by eliminating all federal and state-level restrictions on the procedure. The National Organization for Women explained that the Freedom of Choice Act would "sweep away hundreds of anti-abortion laws [and] policies."[15] Does that sound like someone who's interested in a reduction?

Moreover, you'll notice that, as with dependency and debt, Obama's framing of American notions of choice and freedom are re-imagined to benefit his political agenda. Once a couple has gotten pregnant, whether it was their choice or by accident, a new nascent family member is now part of the discussion. The debate isn't about criminalizing a "choice," it's about criminalizing the destruction of a human being.

Of course, Obama is hardly the first person to believe that abortion is a vital right for American women, but he is certainly the first president to champion the idea that there should be no legal restrictions at all on the procedure. During the 2008 presidential race, he was asked at what point he believed a baby deserved its "human rights." He answered, "whether you're looking at it from a theological perspective or a scientific perspective, answering that question with specificity…is above my pay grade." Unlike many pro-life Americans, I found this answer somewhat refreshing. Humility—even when manufactured—should not be dismissed. But if you don't know when life begins, shouldn't you err on the side of protecting life from the beginning just in case? For Obama, the opposite seemed to be true.

Obama's faux rationality on abortion is undercut by the fact that his record on abortion has always been radical. Most people, it is true, are not very ideological to begin with, often too squeamish to reach decisive conclusions on abortion. They don't want to deal with the reality, and in any event, it's politically incorrect to do so. They balance their views somewhere in the middle. For instance, whatever they think of first-term abortions, a large majority of Americans oppose late-term abortions. But not Obama. In 2003, when he was an Illinois state senator, he stated plainly that he believed abortions should be legal in all situations, even late in a pregnancy:[16]

OBAMA: "I am pro-choice."

REPORTER: "In all situations including the late term thing?"

OBAMA: "I am pro-choice. I believe that women make responsible choices and they know better than anybody the tragedy of a difficult pregnancy and I don't think that it's the government's role to meddle in that choice."

You can't be clearer than that. Obama, who has the state meddling in virtually every aspect of our lives, doesn't want the state to do anything on abortion, except to keep it legal in all circumstances and subsidize it. But surely there has to be a more compelling reason to kill a child who is viable, or mere days from being so, than to say that if a pregnancy is difficult, then it's a tragedy that justifies an abortion. I hate to break it to the president, but most pregnancies are difficult to some extent. Is morning sickness a difficulty strong enough to justify an abortion? Is financial hardship? Is a baby with a disability like Down syndrome a future difficulty to be aborted?

Late-term abortions are rarely needed for purely medical reasons, yet there were around 18,000 late-term abortions performed in this country last year.[17] These are babies—or fetuses, if you like—with advanced neural development, including the ability to feel pain. These are babies who are "viable" outside the womb but are denied the chance to live.

You might remember Kermit Gosnell, the Philadelphia doctor who, among other horrible acts, was killing babies with scissors after "botching" late-term abortions.[18] The doctor, it was reported in 2011, appeared confused by the charges against him at his arraignment. And if you're the kind of guy whose idea of a "botched" medical procedure involves someone surviving, well, perhaps being charged with murder is a distinction without much of a difference. What distinguishes a late-term abortionist from an abortionist who uses scissors to sever the spinal cords of babies born alive is little more than a matter of tools and technique. The results, and the facts, are the same.

Gosnell was charged with his crimes only a week before the president released a celebratory statement for the thirty-eighth anniversary of *Roe v. Wade*, the landmark Supreme Court decision that declared abortion a constitutional right. While the media covered the Gosnell story with horror, Obama hailed "reproductive freedom" as a "fundamental principle."[19] The live-birth procedure favored by Gosnell—delivering fetuses alive and then killing them with a pair of scissors—is illegal, but it wouldn't be if Obama had his way. Our rational president, who lectured religious Americans about "universal values," voted against the Born Alive Infant Protection Act as an Illinois senator. The same senator who voted "present" regularly to avoid other contentious issues took time on four separate occasions to vote against medical care for newborns who survived "botched" late-term abortions.[20] Later, when this became a slight embarrassment, Obama claimed that he would have supported a born-alive act that didn't weaken *Roe v. Wade*—an interesting argument from a politician without any noticeable qualms about weakening the First, Second, Fourth, or Tenth Amendments to the Constitution. As *National Review*'s Ramesh Ponnuru pointed out, the law did nothing more than extend the right to life for babies whom physicians deemed to have "sustainable survivability,"[21] which shouldn't have endangered *Roe v. Wade* at all. Moreover, as a graduate of Harvard Law School, we might expect Obama to know that the Bill of Rights is integral to the Constitution, while *Roe v. Wade*, as even many liberal legal scholars, like his former Harvard professor Laurence Tribe, have confessed, is pretty hard to justify as constitutional law, essentially having been confected out of Justice Harry Blackmun's personal preferences.

After the Sandy Hook Elementary School shooting, where a madman killed 20 children in Newtown, Connecticut, the president gave a heartfelt speech that included this line: "If there is even one step we can take to save another child…then surely we have an obligation to try."[22] Wouldn't one such step be to ban the nihilist practice of murdering children who've survived outside the womb? Obviously, as a state senator, Obama was so ideologically wedded to defending abortion in all circumstances that moderation—if you can call voting to protect a born, living child moderation—was out of the question. As president he shows no signs of changing his views—in fact, his hardline position on abortion is now Democratic Party dogma.

Party at the End of the World

At the 2012 Democratic National Convention in Charlotte, North Carolina, Democrats threw themselves all in for abortion. No longer were they hesitant to embrace death as a political tool. No longer did they keep a veneer of diversity of opinion on the issue. In Charlotte, the head of NARAL Pro-Choice America argued that being allowed to have free abortions on demand was the realization of the American Dream.

A woman whose only claim to fame was demanding free condoms and abortions was celebrated as a hero. In her speech, abortion and taxpayer-funded-contraception activist Sandra Fluke, who had learned much from Obama in inverting logic, despicably accused vice presidential candidate Paul Ryan of supporting a bill that "would allow pregnant women to die preventable deaths in our emergency rooms." Actually, what Ryan had done was support a measure that would have reinstated into Obamacare conscience protections for pro-life medical workers who might otherwise be coerced into assisting in practices they deem immoral, or have to quit their jobs.[23]

Another woman named Libby Bruce told delegates how Planned Parenthood, the nation's largest abortion provider, had treated her endometriosis 12 years ago—because, apparently, Republicans opposed treating endometriosis and Planned Parenthood was the only organization in the country that could treat it.

President Obama "believes that women are more than capable of making our own choices about our bodies and our health care," said the First Lady to grand cheers, except of course that through Obamacare the administration was dictating a good many of our choices and asking that we subsidize other people's choices.

A one-time supposed Republican, Maria Ciano, assured the crowd that if voters were kind enough to give the president a second term, "our right to make our own most personal decisions will be safe for another generation." By "our," it should be noted, Ciano did not mean the more than one million unborn children every year who will never enjoy making any decisions at all.

Abortion was mentioned—explicitly or indirectly—in many speeches those three days. A number of speakers based their entire case for Obama's reelection on the fact that Obama would protect the right to dispose of human life. Was this really the most vital issue to voters? For anyone who understood what these advocates were really fighting for, the Democratic Convention was a jarring experience. Its speakers put together a collage of progressive ideals that equated to a future, by any rational analysis, of bankruptcy, state dependency, state coercion, and imaginary rights (to state-provided contraception and abortion, among other things). The speakers outlined a future where we didn't have to shoulder much personal responsibility—the state would take care of everything by taxing the rich—and expressed a sort of unnerving joy in the right to abort children. This was, as it turns out, rather appealing to the majority of American voters.

Nancy Keenan, for instance, the president of one of the nation's largest pro-abortion groups, NARAL Pro-Choice America, attacked Republican hopeful Mitt Romney. "Put simply, women in America cannot trust Mitt Romney," she said. "We cannot trust Mitt Romney to protect our health. He would repeal Obamacare, taking away our access to better maternity and prenatal care, and the law's near universal coverage of birth control. And we cannot trust Mitt Romney to respect our rights."[24]

Do we, as Americans, really believe that the president's job is to "protect" our health? Do we really believe that taxpayers should pay for better maternity and prenatal care? Do we really believe that taxpayers should pony up for universal coverage of birth control? Apparently we do. But if maternity, prenatal care, and birth control are deeply personal matters between a woman and a doctor, then why is the government coercing taxpayers into the doctor's office? Leftists, of course, love expanding the state, but the president of NARAL had a very specific goal in mind. She was muddling an array of progressive issues in order to expand abortion rights and taxpayer-subsidized abortions.

Democrats have transformed their party from one that supports abortion rights to one that considers state promotion of abortion central to America's future. In 2008 and 2012, Democrats expunged the word "rare" from the party platform when it came to abortion. After all, if abortion is one of the most "fundamental rights" Americans possess, why should it be rare and why should it be restricted? At least the Democrats have become more ideologically consistent. The Democratic platform went on to support a woman's "right" to choose an abortion without mentioning any exceptions for partial-birth or late-term abortions and put in writing that abortion was a right deserving of taxpayer subsidies:[25]

> The Democratic Party strongly and unequivocally supports *Roe v. Wade* and a woman's right to make decisions regarding her pregnancy, including a safe and legal abortion, regardless of ability to pay. We oppose any and all efforts to weaken or undermine that right. Abortion is an intensely personal decision between a woman, her family, her doctor, and her clergy; there is no place for politicians or government to get in the way.

Isn't putting the nation's entire health care industry under government control an example of "politicians or government" getting "in the way"? And when the Democrats declare that abortion is a right "regardless of ability to pay," they don't mean that the Democratic National Committee is going to set aside a checking account to pay for hundreds of thousands of abortions. They meant the "government" should pay. They were talking about you, the taxpayer. When you file your taxes and see how much the federal government has extracted from your work, do you get a warm, glowing feeling that some of your money went to ensure the death of unborn children?

Admittedly, Republicans didn't help their cause in 2012 with a couple of poorly reasoned and highly offensive comments that allowed Obama to turn the abortion issue back on the GOP. Republican Senate candidate Todd Akin in Missouri made an especially egregious mess of things when he was asked if he supported an abortion exemption for victims of rape. "From what I understand from doctors," he answered, "that's really rare. If it's a legitimate rape, the female body has ways to try to shut that whole thing down. But let's assume that maybe that didn't work or something. I think there should be some punishment."[26]

Akin later backpedaled, saying he "misspoke" with "off-the-cuff remarks." But, as a rule of thumb, whenever a politician drops the words "legitimate" and "rape" in tandem that politician has already lost whatever argument he's in—and, in this case, he did considerable political damage to the pro-life cause and his party. It didn't matter that a Romney spokesperson immediately told CBS News, "Governor Romney and Congressman Ryan disagree with Mr. Akin's statement, and a Romney-Ryan administration would not oppose abortion in instances of rape." Nor did it matter that Romney told *National Review* that Akin's comments were "inexcusable." The Obama campaign repeatedly connected Akin to Romney, to the GOP (which repudiated its own candidate), and to the pro-life movement as a whole, making the abortion issue work in its favor.

What should frustrate pro-lifers most about people who use pseudoscientific gibberish to make pro-life arguments is that pro-lifers already have science on their side. Akin could have simply answered: rape is a brutal crime, but compounding one tragedy with another does not undo the horrifying act. Although cases of pregnancy from rape and incest are rare, that doesn't make the suffering of the victims any less devastating. But it also doesn't change the fact that the vast majority of abortions are performed for the sake of convenience. Science unequivocally tells us we are dealing with a vulnerable new life. How we deal with that new life says a lot about our morality. If pro-life candidates spoke with confidence, which they rarely do, being intimidated by liberals and the mainstream media, then perhaps Obama's gibberish would start to sink in.

"I don't know how these guys come up with these ideas," Obama told Jay Leno on *The Tonight Show*. "These various distinctions about rape don't make too much sense to me; don't make any sense to me."[27] The president was referencing Akin, but also Richard Mourdock, the Indiana Republican senatorial candidate who ignited his own controversy by asserting that pregnancies resulting from rape are "something that God intended to happen."

Mourdock had clumsily tried to make the point that even through tragedy and evil God can create good. Surely, even liberals might agree with such an innocuous sentiment—but not when there is political gain to be made. To Obama, voting against saving the life of a baby born through a botched abortion is simply good sense. If that baby survived it might be a standing rebuke to abortion rights. That a baby conceived in a rape is still a human life is something that a backwoods hick can understand, but that is beyond the comprehension of our sophisticated, well-educated president.

Obama and the progressive Democrats used their slick and nimble marketing operation to make the Republicans look like radicals, but by the standards of American public opinion, it is the Democrats who are the extremists on abortion. Most Americans, if you believe polls, deem abortion morally wrong, even if it is legal. Most Americans believe late-term abortions should be banned. Most Americans believe in parental consent in the case of a minor. Most believe that a married woman should notify her husband before procuring an abortion. Most claim to oppose the use of public funds to pay for anyone's abortion. Obama opposed every single one of those regulations, yet he was never framed as the radical on the issue. That should worry us more than anything.

Family Un-Planning

If, as Obama argues, abortion is one of our most fundamental rights, then of course, to the progressive mind, a lack of money can't stand in the way of enjoying that right. As we don't quite have nationalized health care yet, this can be achieved in two ways: 1) by funneling taxpayer money to organizations that offer abortions, and 2) by forcing the private sector to offer abortions to all citizens.

Addressing a crowd of supporters at the Oregon Convention Center during the 2012 presidential campaign, President Barack Obama erected one of his standard straw men, claiming, "Mr. Romney wants to get rid of funding for Planned Parenthood. I think that's a bad idea. I've got two daughters. I want them to control their own health care choices."[28]

Actually, Mr. Romney had proposed cutting government funding for Planned Parenthood because doing so would have freed millions of Americans from the burden of funding an organization they find morally repugnant. But Obama, a millionaire, believed that others should subsidize his daughters' choices, and he made no distinction about how we fund organizations.

In 2009–10, Planned Parenthood received $487.4 million in government grants, contracts, and reimbursements.[29] Over Obama's first term, government funding for Planned Parenthood jumped from about a third of the organization's budget to more than 45 percent. Pro-choice activists like to argue that abortions constitute a mere 3 percent of Planned Parenthood's services, but they neglect to mention that abortion accounts for at least a third of Planned Parenthood's total income from clinic services.

Abortion advocates also like to claim that taxpayer dollars do not directly fund abortion. They have to say this because such funding is technically illegal under the Hyde Amendment that bars the use of federal funds to pay for abortions (with exceptions for incest and rape). But since the government dollars given to Planned Parenthood are fungible, millions of taxpayers have contributed to a procedure they view as murder. Planned Parenthood, in fact, reported performing 329,445 abortions in 2010.

Taxpayers are not only forced to fund Planned Parenthood, they have to pay for pro-abortion groups to support pro-abortion politicians. Planned Parenthood spent $12 million on the 2012 presidential election through its political action committees. It was a wise investment. Not surprisingly, given Obama's support for Planned Parenthood, that's more money than it has ever spent in an election. The Associated Press reported that around half of the money was spent on television ads in such battleground states as Florida, Ohio, and Virginia—all won by Obama. Dawn Laguens, executive vice president of Planned Parenthood, said the organization deserved a huge amount of credit for Obama's reelection. Their taxpayer-funded scaremongering was meant to make voters doubt Romney and help an unpopular president. Planned Parenthood hoped to expand "the amount of time they [voters] were willing to give the president and the economy to recover. So we could kind of hold them in 'undecided' by, in particularly in the presidency, by making Mitt Romney questionable in their mind on our set of issues."[30]

To recap: money from taxpayers goes to a group they find objectionable. That group, in turn, funds politicians who are then elected and procure more funding—and more campaign cash.

This obviously corrupt relationship has led many state legislators to explore ways to defund Planned Parenthood. In some states, like Indiana, courts have stepped in to stop the legislative efforts. In other states, the Obama administration did the trick. In 2012, for instance, the North Carolina legislature passed a budget adjustment bill that redirected $343,000 away from Planned Parenthood to county health departments that provide comprehensive care for women rather than abortions. So what did the Obama administration do? They awarded $426,000 in federal grants to Planned Parenthood affiliates in North Carolina.[31]

When fully implemented, the Affordable Care Act, widely known as Obamacare, will be the most effective way to divert tax dollars to abortionists. Already Obamacare promises to fund "community health centers," often run by our friends at Planned Parenthood. That's just the beginning of how the government plans to expand abortion in America.

The few remaining pro-life Democrats in the House, you might remember, held up Obamacare briefly; most of them, incidentally, are gone now. Obama cut a deal that, if they would set aside their moral concerns about abortion and vote for the bill, he would promise to sign an Executive Order to ensure that federal funds were not used for abortion services. The president said, "This is a healthcare bill, not an abortion bill."[32]

As it turns out, it is both, and the executive order did nothing but get Obama the congressional votes he needed. Not only does Obamacare offer federal subsidies to groups that provide abortions, but it also subsidizes health care plans that cover elective abortions.

Catholicism Not Required

Nat Hentoff once remarked that when he turned pro-life, his journalistic cohorts wondered when he had "converted to Catholicism—the only explanation they could think of" for his "apostasy."

I am not a convert to Catholicism either. But you don't have to be a Catholic to see how Obamacare and its mandate requiring insurers to cover contraception and abortifacients is a direct attack on religious freedom. We should all be afraid when progressive notions of "reproductive rights" kick the Constitution—a document that features some fundamental rights of its own—to the curb.

When it comes to appointing justices to the Supreme Court, liberals always insist that conservatives should impose no "litmus" tests, by which they mean that conservatives would be wrong to insist on pro-life justices. Yet, when a Democratic president is in office, it is automatically assumed that any Supreme Court justice will have passed the liberals' own litmus test of defending *Roe v. Wade*. Likewise, liberals like to pose as defenders of the First Amendment, but they are very selective about what they choose to defend. When it comes to freedom of religious expression and freedom of conscience that contradict their belief in abortion, they are not so sympathetic. To Obama progressives, religious institutions are, in fact, the greatest threat to state-mandated abortion coverage. The leftists have put the federal government and the Catholic Church on a collision course of exactly the sort the Founding Fathers designed the Constitution to avoid.

An entire book could be written on what little regard the Obama administration has for religious freedom.[33] But here are two striking examples. In 2009, the American Civil Liberties Union of Massachusetts sued the United States Department of Health and Human Services to eliminate federal grants to Catholic charities that were aiding the victims of human trafficking. The ACLU alleged that such public support amounted to an establishment of religion. Before the ruling was even offered, the HHS had cut off funding to the group. The federal government announced that it was going to give preference to grantees, not on the basis of who did the most effective job of helping the poor and suffering, but on the basis of whether the grantees offered "the full range of legally permissible gynecological and obstetric care"—meaning, of course, abortion.

On January 20, 2012, the Department of Health and Human Services under Secretary Kathleen Sebelius initiated a new policy which required nearly all private health insurance plans to include coverage for contraceptive drugs and devices, surgical sterilizations, and abortion-inducing drugs. This was the first example of how Obamacare could be used to coerce Americans into funding progressive aims. The Catholic Church believes that contraception, sterilization, and abortion are morally wrong. Whatever you make of abortifacient drugs, forcing Catholics (or anyone) to fund their dissemination clearly undermines the First Amendment.

When the Catholic Church argues that contraception and abortion go hand in hand, most people scoff, because most people, myself included, still think the former might help prevent the latter. But the Obama administration has proven that Catholic Church right in at least this regard: once the state gets in the business of deciding that contraception or abortion are moral goods, not only will the state guarantee their existence, it will fund them, and it will do so in ways that are ever more coercive and restrictive of religious freedom.

It was rather amazing to watch the hubris of the Obama administration as it made its case for Obamacare and the contraception mandate. It was a case that required at least three parts. First, the administration had to argue that the government has the power to force every adult to purchase a product in the private marketplace (in this case, health insurance through Obamacare). Second, it insisted that the government could require companies to provide products within this market (in this case, contraception and morning-after pills). Finally, it demanded that everyone—including Catholic business owners and Catholic institutions—must subsidize these products even if they find them morally objectionable and at odds with their religious beliefs. When we talk here about religious freedom, make no mistake that we're also talking about individual freedom. The Obama administration's decision to force Catholic institutions to pay for and offer (directly or indirectly) products the Church considers immoral is an assault on religious freedom and freedom of conscience. For a secular person it should also underline the importance of consumer choice. After all, when government dictates what people buy and sell, it dictates much more. When the state creates virtual monopolies through regulatory regimes, it also gets to decide what is moral and necessary, and it compels everyone to act accordingly. Obama's attack on religious freedom is also an attack on economic freedom; in fact, when the state attacks one of our guaranteed liberties, it almost invariably leads to attacks on others.

It was, as it turns out, Democrats who argued that contraception and abortion were inseparable issues under the rubric of "reproductive health." They did so because contraception is far more popular than abortion. By creating false fears that Republicans threatened legalized contraception, Democrats generated public support to force institutions into providing abortion funding (as well as subsidized contraception under Obamacare). Never mind that not a single Republican had called for banning contraception. Never mind that not even the Catholic Church advocated banning contraception or sterilization drugs. The Church just wanted to follow its own long-established beliefs which we had all managed to tolerate in America until Obama came along. Now liberals argued that religious institutions were attempting to deny women access to these drugs, as if the Church had a moral, financial, and legal obligation to provide them.

Soon after the issue blew up, Obama claimed the controversy was "an issue where people of goodwill on both sides of the debate have been sorting through some very complicated questions to find a solution that works for everyone."[34] Which is pure rubbish, of course. Obama, a man unwilling to compromise on legislation that would have saved babies from botched abortions, knew full well that Catholics don't really have much wiggle room on the mortal sin front. Nor was the "question" complicated. Obama made it complicated to further his ideological goals.

The Protestant presidents of Colorado Christian University, Louisiana College, and Geneva College offered their own convincing argument against Obama's "sin" tax in a *Wall Street Journal* op-ed:[35]

> This "conscience tax" is a blatant violation of the freedoms of religion and speech guaranteed by the U.S. Constitution and affirmed by federal laws such as the Religious Freedom Restoration Act. This mandate would be unjust even if it applied only to those who accept government funding, but it does much more than that. It applies to private, religious employers just because they exist in American society, regardless of whether they receive government funding.

Without many choices left, the University of Notre Dame (where Obama once spoke, despite his views on abortion), the Archdiocese of New York, the Catholic University of America, the dioceses serving Dallas and Pittsburgh, the archdioceses of St. Louis and Washington, D.C., and dozens of other Roman Catholic institutions sued the Obama administration in federal court. "The government…cannot justify its decision to force Notre Dame to provide, pay for, and/or facilitate access to these services in violation of its sincerely held religious beliefs," Notre Dame's lawsuit argues. "If the government can force religious institutions to violate their beliefs in such a manner, there is no apparent limit to the government's power."

But that, of course, was the point.

The Obama administration ostensibly offered a conscience clause for religious organizations, but it was a joke. So slender was this reed that nearly all religious institutions providing health, educational, or charitable services would not have been unable to qualify for protection from government interference. As plaintiffs in the suit liked to point out, Jesus and the apostles wouldn't have qualified for the exemption. But that, again, was the point. The Obama administration had no intention of allowing exceptions. It had hoped to browbeat Catholic institutions into compliance. Now it would try and set a new precedent through the courts. This tactic may finally backfire. Judge Brian Cogan, in an Eastern District Federal Court decision allowing the Catholic suits to move forward, rejected the Obama administration's arguments in favor of its mandates, calling the administration's steps against the religious institutions an "actual and well-founded fear" that is "looming and certain" much like "a speeding train that is coming towards plaintiffs." Then Judge Cogan wrote this wonderful sentence: "The First Amendment does not require citizens to accept assurances from the government that, if the government later determines it has made a misstep, it will take ameliorative action."

Tomorrow's Children

Though Democrats groused endlessly that Republicans were attempting to snatch their reproductive rights, it was the Obama administration that was attempting to snuff out any dissent to anti-reproductive rights. It might be one thing for the state to sanction and subsidize the taking of a human life in executions for heinous criminals, or in fighting a war. But an unborn child has not been convicted of any crime. An unborn child is not a foreign enemy. When the state advances the elimination of human lives as a human right and provides subsidies for it simply because those lives are inconvenient, we're talking about a special kind of state-sponsored nihilism.

We devalue all life through abortion. You may not consider a fetus a "human life" in early pregnancy, even though it has its own DNA and medical science continues to find ways to keep the fetus viable outside the womb earlier and earlier. It's difficult to understand how those who harp on the importance of "science" in public policy can draw an arbitrary timeline in the pregnancy, defining when human life is worth saving and when it can be terminated.

What happens when abortion begins to transform from a type of birth control to a type of eugenics? A few years ago, *Newsweek* reported that 90 percent of women whose fetuses test positive for Down syndrome choose to abort.[36] Another survey showed that only a small percentage of mothers even used the test. So what happens when 90 percent of parents test their fetuses? Does it mean the end of the disorder, or are we stepping perilously close to even more nihilistic behavior? What about future DNA tests that can detect any defects in a fetus? What happens when we can use abortion to weed out the blind, the mentally ill, the ugly, or any other "undesirable" human beings?

Recently, Sweden's National Board of Health and Welfare ruled that women are permitted to abort their children based on the sex of the fetuses. Sex-selection abortions are a growing trend here as well. In 2012, the Republican-controlled House voted down a measure that would have imposed fines and prison terms on doctors who perform sex-selection abortions. Of course, doctors and mothers would have been able to lie about it, and admittedly, I'm not sure why terminating the fetus because it's the wrong sex is any worse than terminating the fetus for convenience's sake. The fate of the fetus does not change; only the reasoning for its extinction does. In the United States, a woman can have an abortion for nearly any reason she chooses. In fact, a health exemption for the mother allows abortions to be performed virtually on demand. If you oppose selective abortions but not abortion overall, it is only because the idea transforms an abstract proposition into a choice that has consequences. If one used progressive logic on abortion, there would be no leeway for regulations on why or who is terminated, because abortion has nothing to do with the baby and everything to do with the mother's choices.

As much as it upsets liberals to bring this up, Margaret Sanger, the founder of Planned Parenthood, was not only a racist but was also a proponent of weeding out undesirables. She was interested in discouraging the "unfit" and "inferior" from reproducing. In her 1922 book, *The Pivot of Civilization,* Sanger advocated for the segregation of "morons, misfits, and the maladjusted" and the sterilization of "genetically inferior races." She was also behind the Negro Project, the first major undertaking of the new Birth Control Federation of America.[37]

That's not to say that the pro-choice advocates of Planned Parenthood are all racists—not intentionally, at least. Still, it is undeniable that African American and Hispanic women account for a disproportionate share of abortions. Put it this way: around 41 percent of all New York City pregnancies end in abortion—a tragedy in itself. Broken down by race, non-Hispanic blacks have a 59.8 percent abortion rate in New York City, Hispanics have a 41.3 percent abortion rate, Asians have a 22.7 percent abortion rate, and non-Hispanic whites have a 20.4 percent abortion rate.[38]

Since the abortion industry targets black women and Latinas, those numbers should be expected. Planned Parenthood constructs most of its abortion clinics in minority neighborhoods. A recent study shows that nearly 80 percent of Planned Parenthood's surgical abortion facilities are located within walking distance of African American or Latino communities.[39] According to the National Vital Statistics Report in late 2012, African American women experience an average of 1.6 times more pregnancies than white women, but have 5 times more abortions over their lifetime.[40] In Fiscal Year 2009–2010, according to Planned Parenthood's annual report, 40 percent of the 329,445 abortions performed took the lives of minority babies.[41]

People Are a Disease

Obama was not content with pushing abortion as a fundamental right here at home. He is in favor of American taxpayers subsidizing it abroad as well. In 2010, Secretary of State Hillary Clinton announced that the United States would fund efforts to promote "reproductive health care and family planning" as a "basic right" around the world. This push included abortion, naturally. The plan would move funding from programs that had been earmarked for HIV/AIDS, tuberculosis, and malaria prevention to population control. Speaking at the International Conference on Population and Development in Cairo, Clinton promised to help ensure that "all governments will make access to reproductive health care and family-planning services a basic right."[42] Citizens of countries where freedom of assembly, religion, and speech are still a dream were no doubt a bit perplexed by the Obama administration's idea of a basic right.

But it wasn't surprising. It took the president only three days in office to repeal the pro-life "Mexico City Policy."[43] Under that policy, the U.S. government was banned from funding any euphemistic "family planning services" that provided abortions. Ronald Reagan had introduced the legislation in 1984 in Mexico City. It was overturned by President Bill Clinton in 1993 and restored by George W. Bush in 2001.

Not only do progressives believe abortion is a positive good both at home and abroad, but they often believe it is a necessity to stem the danger of overpopulation. For decades, the Sierra Club and other environmentalist groups have warned us that too many babies will destroy the earth. "We are experiencing an accelerated obliteration of the planet's life-forms—an estimated 8,760 species die off per year—because, simply put, there are too many people," explained environmentalist Chris Hedges, a Pulitzer Prize-winning reporter. Al Gore, former vice president, Nobel Prize winner, and filmmaker, constantly argues that there are too many people soiling the earth. "One of the things that we could do about it is to change the technologies," he explained at the Games for Change Festival in 2010, "to put out less of this pollution, to stabilize the population, and one of the principal ways of doing that is to empower and educate girls and women. You have to have ubiquitous availability of fertility management so women can choose how many children [they] have, the spacing of the children."

The *New York Times*' Thomas Friedman asked, "How did we not panic when the evidence was so obvious that we'd crossed some growth/climate/natural resource/population redlines all at once?"

Perhaps some of us didn't panic because we believe in the ability of humans to adapt and to innovate. Perhaps we've learned that Malthusian Chicken Littles have been proved so wrong so often that we've finally begun to ignore them. Perhaps we have come to recognize that the world's greatest resource is in fact creative people working to solve problems.

You might also remember that in a *New York Times* interview, Supreme Court Justice Ruth Bader Ginsburg let slip that she "thought that at the time *Roe* [*v. Wade*] was decided, there was concern about population growth and particularly growth in populations that we don't want to have too many of." How delightful!

The Obama administration did their small part, sending a $50 million check to the United Nations Population Fund, a pro-abortion group that has been accused of tacitly supporting Chinese family planning policies—you know, a one-child policy that includes forced abortions and sterilizations and other human rights. The Bush administration had withheld the funds because of this unsavory alliance, but Obama signed a bill to reverse the Bush policy. Perhaps this was done on the advice of Obama's "science czar," John Holdren, co-author (with Paul Ehrlich of *Population Bomb* notoriety) of a book in the 1970s that toyed with the idea of compulsory sterilization and coerced abortions—to "de-develop the United States."

Holdren, director of the White House Office of Science and Technology Policy, is a longtime prophet of environmental catastrophes from population explosions. Thanks to resourceful bloggers, you can read excerpts online from his hard-to-find book, *Ecoscience: Population, Resources, and Environment*. In it, Holdren ponders how "population-control laws, even including laws requiring compulsory abortion, could be sustained under the existing Constitution." The book is sprinkled with comparable statements that passively discuss how coercive population control methods might rescue the world from…well, humans. When I called Holdren's office, I was told that the czar "does not now and never has been an advocate of compulsory abortions or other repressive measures to limit fertility." A lie.

Holdren also participated in the famous wager between overpopulation theorist Paul Ehrlich and economist Julian Simon. Simon believed that human ingenuity would triumph over any presumed scarcity of natural resources. He challenged Ehrlich to pick five natural resources that he thought would experience shortages and whose prices would consequently rise over the course of at least a year. Ehrlich, and Holdren who helped advise him, chose five metals and said their prices would be higher ten years later. Ehrlich lost the bet on all counts, as the composite price index for the commodities he picked, like copper and chromium, fell by more than 40 percent.

Today, while Holdren has publicly tempered his aversion to population growth, he still advocates that the government nudge us toward having fewer children. Instead of coercion, though, he is a fan of "motivation." When Holdren was asked during his Senate confirmation hearing about his penchant for scientific overstatements, he responded, "The motivation for looking at the downside possibilities, the possibilities that can go wrong if things continue in a bad direction, is to motivate people to change direction. That was my intention at the time." Holdren's past flies in the face of Obama's contention, made on the day of the science czar's appointment, that his administration was "ensuring that facts and evidence are never twisted or obscured by politics or ideology."

But that's another story.

Intolerance

There are consequences to the pro-life position, of course. Certainly an unwanted baby, a mentally anguished mother, and the prospect of a back-alley abortion are real-world problems. Certainly restricting abortion doesn't solve all the problems, as women will still seek out providers illegally. The pro-lifer will typically be sympathetic to these concerns. If Americans want to reduce the number of abortions there will have to be a broader conversation about policy, but that's not going to happen, because the Obama administration has successfully portrayed pro-lifers as ignorant enemies of progress. So there will be no real conversation about abortion. And there won't be one for a very long time.

Americans will find it harder to take an honest look at the issue, because of the cultural and political baggage Obama and the progressives have hung on it. They have made it very difficult for a person of secular sensibilities to be pro-life because they have painted the pro-life position as a religious one, without any grounding in science or reason, grounded instead in old prejudices that merely oppress and demean women. This portrait of pro-lifers existed before Obama, but he has put it on a much broader canvas, and it seems undeniable that it successfully distracted many Americans from what abortion is really about.

If the president's leadership matters to young people as much as we are led to believe, millions of Millennials will now view terminating a pregnancy—once considered at best a terrible choice and at worst killing—as a choice without much moral consequence. They will see it as a fundamental right bestowed on them by government. Of course, most people still make these choices under tremendous stress and heartbreak, and many others will regret their decision for the rest of their lives. Under Obama, and moving forward, many more will feel that anguish.

And millions more will never feel anything.

CHAPTER SIX

FOR WHOM THE BELL TOLLS

"The cost of living was not lowered, but profitable employment, the only means wherewith the people could meet any cost, reached well nigh the point of disappearance.

The charge laid against Republicans of countenancing the wicked principle of putting the dollar above the man, was entirely outdone by the Democratic practice, which put the dollar completely out of reach of the man.

The industrial line vanished and the bread line increased. Organized charity and government had to relieve unemployment. We were told that this was 'mostly psychological.' It was. Men had thoroughly grasped the idea that there was not only no profit in attempting to carry on the business of the nation, but that it was looked upon with suspicion, and when successful was likely to be indicted as a crime."

—Calvin Coolidge,
Tremont Temple, Boston, September 1920

It Tolls for Thee

It is probably too late to evade the disasters laid out in this book. We'll have to deal with them, and perhaps doing so sooner rather than later is best. Who knows? Conceivably we'll emerge stronger and freer. Certainly, for those of us who value liberty, it's worth fighting. For now, the chief problem is that Americans who believe in classical liberalism, practical libertarianism, and traditional conservatism are in political retreat.

Part of the problem, of course, is that we're stuck with the impotent and clueless Republican Party, which has long ago abandoned the principles of fiscal conservatism, and now, even as it tries to do the right thing, simply doesn't have the political acumen to compete with the president. When you consider what Obama might try to do in a second term, and how feeble the Republican opposition is in Congress, you might well think that, as this book argues, we are in for a rough ride with the four horsemen of the apocalypse.

Spread the Wealth

"Somebody helped to create this unbelievable American system that we have that allowed you to thrive," Obama claimed in a rousing 2012 campaign speech to a crowd in Roanoke, Virginia. Once a state of conservative Democrats and even more conservative Republicans, Virginia is now a swing state that Obama has won twice. "Somebody invested in roads and bridges. If you've got a business—you didn't build that. Somebody else made that happen. The Internet didn't get invented on its own."[1]

Republicans, rightly, rejected the president's contention that Americans hadn't built their own businesses and were simply fortunate enough to be propped up by government's kindness. This was a worthy bone to pick with the president—though it was hardly a surprising comment from him. The truly creepy part of Obama's statement was his broader conception of the "unbelievable American system."

Obama has it all backwards. It is the charity of a prosperous free society that allows people to become community organizers or attain "free" health care. Washington rarely helps the free market prosper, but a prosperous private sector is what allows Washington to throw billions of dollars into unproductive but morally pleasing projects—stimuli, research, and dependency programs favored by the president. Society needs the rule of law to function, not a progressive policy czar eager to reshape the country.

Then it dawned on me that Obama's "unbelievable American system" was actually his own idea of America.

There are two strains of thought that drive modern progressive policy—both are forms of authoritarianism—which make any escape from the four impending economic and moral calamities unrealistic and the prospect of deeper agony a very real possibility.

The first strain, encompassing economic and social choices, is the belief that the state is better suited than private citizens to allocate funds and to direct how, why, and when citizens make their economic decisions. These policies manifest themselves in the Nanny State or in Obamacare or in "green" regulations that direct economic behavior and restrict economic liberty. These days liberals advocate for restrictions on nearly every aspect of economic life, from where you buy health care, to what kind of health care you buy, to where you send your kids to school, to what kind of car you drive, to what sort of energy you put in the car, to what kind of light bulbs you can turn on, to what kind of food you should give your kids…and that's just for starters. Nearly all these intrusions are given a halo of virtue that makes them appealing to many Americans. What left-wing budget isn't based on the "morality" of spending or the immorality of cutting some cherished—at least to certain congressmen and their special interest constituency—program? For all the talk about the Religious Right seeking to impose their morality on people, it's the progressives who have done this, not conservatives. In fact, as is immediately obvious to any clear-eyed viewer of American politics, Republican politicians fear and shy away from moral arguments. The left doesn't. And that's one reason why they win. The left has convinced a great swath of the electorate that the liberal arguments are the moral arguments. Liberals are so successful at this that even many Republicans think that's the case, which is why they strive to be "compassionate" conservatives or media-approved "moderates" or, like Mitt Romney, take positions that make Reagan-era conservatives cringe—such as affirming that *of course* the federal government has a role to play in education.

Progressives have such certitude in their ethical superiority that it leads to the second main strain of progressive thought, which can be captured in the old adage that the ends justify the means (something, by the way, which classical philosophers like Aristotle denied, as did classical Christianity as embodied in the teachings of the Catholic Church).

It is no coincidence that even though he had a congressional majority for half of his first term, the Obama administration has acted as if the greatest crisis of American democracy is that the president could not always get his own way. Since Obama is doing what is morally right, they reason, nothing should impede his progress.

When immigration policy was not moving forward, Senate Majority Leader Harry Reid argued that the president was free to unilaterally craft policy because "we've tried to do that for years, and we can't because they [the Republicans] won't let us." For those of you who have forgotten, in the *Federalist Papers*, Publius writes, "In a republic, all the power surrendered by the people is submitted to the administration of a single government; and the usurpations are guarded against by a division of the government into distinct and separate departments."[2] There is no addendum that says: "but if they don't let you do what you want, feel free to disregard the previous statement."

Whenever Congress is unable to pass progressive agenda items with a simple majority of legislators, the vote of a single person will do just fine. President Obama once said, "We can't wait for Congress to do its job. So where they won't act, I will. We're going to look every single day to figure out what we can do without Congress."[3]

One might forgive a little autocratic hyperbole in the heat of a campaign season, but Obama flexed executive power whenever possible. He circumvented Congress on college loans and mortgages. He directed the Justice Department to stop defending the Defense of Marriage Act. Through rulemaking, he empowered the Environmental Protection Agency to effectively institute legislation that Democrats could not pass. Obama invoked executive privilege in the Fast and Furious gunrunning investigation regarding documents that he supposedly knew nothing about.

He involved the United States in military action in Libya without congressional consent and installed four recess appointments without bothering to wait for Congress to recess. No president had ever made a recess appointment while the Senate was still in session until President Obama appointed Richard Cordray to serve as director of the Consumer Financial Protection Bureau.

Then, Obama made the decision to grant 800,000 young illegal immigrants a reprieve from deportation, undoing a perfectly legitimate legislative deadlock by simply ignoring the law.

Granted, Obama isn't the first president to issue executive orders or expand and abuse the power of the presidency, but he seems on track to be the worst, and with fewer scruples. Getting things done is an imperative for the Obama administration. But getting things done really isn't the role of government; it's the role of businesses and of private charities. The role of government is to defend the United States and uphold the rule of law. People who care about the Constitution and liberty don't want a president who "gets things done;" we want a president who obeys the Constitution he has sworn to uphold.

Obama's Four Horsemen are coming. The only way we're going to be able to survive them is if conservatives can pull it together and remind the American people who we are as Americans, where we came from out of the classical liberal ideals of the revolution, and what we stand for as a beacon of freedom and hope. The real moral high ground is ours. We need to reclaim it.

ACKNOWLEDGMENTS

I n a world of unknowns one thing is certain: someone important is going to be left out of my acknowledgments. Whoever you are, I'm sorry.

It would be difficult to forget Harry Crocker, who brought me the idea and oversaw the entire process (though any errors, zealotry, poorly convinced arguments, etc., are mine alone). I'm greatly appreciative of Marji Ross, Maria Ruhl, Tess Civantos, Alberto Rojas, Brittany Roh, Ryan Pando, Rebekah Meinecke, and everyone at Regnery for their great speed, precision, and dedication.

Thanks, also, to Jeff Carneal for his trust and guidance.

Without Cathy Taylor and Joe Guerriero, there would have been no book—so feel free to blame them as well. It's been great working with the talented group at *Human Events*—Karl Selzer, Adam Tragone, John Hayward, Audrey Hudson, Hope Hodge, Neil McCabe, and John Gizzi. Tom Winter and Allan Ryskind always keep me on my toes.

Thanks also to Kevin Balfe, Glenn Beck, Michelle Malkin, Fred Barnes, Jonah Goldberg, David Yontz, Jim Pfaff, Brad Cohan, Harris Vederman, and David Pietrusza.

Boaz, Oren, Anne, MK, Eva, and Jim, I appreciate your support. Hannah, Noah, Szerena, Amanda, Dylan, and Lydia: Good luck. You're going to need it. Thanks also to Paul for letting me bounce ideas off him. Theresa, thanks for all your encouragement over the years. Rest in peace, Paul.

Though these days ideas like "liberty" might be ridiculed as jejune, Mom and Dad risked everything for them. I can never thank them enough.

To my wife Carla, supportive and loving even in the face of never-ending cantankerous rants, and to Adria and Leah, I love you all.

NOTES

Chapter 2

1. "Life of Julia," BarackObama.com, http://www.barackobama.com/life-of-julia/.

2. Stephan Holmes and Cass R. Sunstein, "Why We Should Celebrate Paying Taxes," *Chicago Tribune*, April 14, 1999, http://home.uchicago.edu/~csunstei/celebrate.html.

3. U.S Department of Health & Human Services, "Head Start Impact Study and Follow-up, 2000-2012," Office of Planning, Research and Evaluation, January 15, 2010, http://www.acf.hhs.gov/programs/opre/research/project/head-start-impact-study-and-follow-up-2000-2012.

4. "NHSA applauds $2.1 billion in economic recovery package for Head Start/Early Head Start," National Head Start Association press release, November 15, 2009, http://www.nhsa.org/news_release_1152009. Richard Alleyne, "Young adults believe in the age of entitlement, claim researchers," *Telegraph*, May 24, 2010, http://www.telegraph.co.uk/news/uknews/7760687/Young-adults-believe-in-the-age-of-entitlement-claim-researchers.html.

5. Richard Alleyne, "Young adults believe in the age of entitlement, claim researchers," *Telegraph*, May 24, 2010, http://www.telegraph.co.uk/news/uknews/7760687/Young-adults-believe-in-the-age-of-entitlement-claim-researchers.html.

6. Kathy Warbelow and Frank Bass, "Young U.S. Adults Flock to Parents' Homes Amid Economy," Bloomberg, September 25, 2012, http://www.bloomberg.com/news/2012-09-25/young-adults-flock-to-parents-homes-amid-sour-economy.html.

7. Kim Parker, "The Boomerang Generation," Pew Social & Demographic Trends, March 15, 2012, http://www.pewsocialtrends.org/2012/03/15/the-boomerang-generation/.

8. Cheryl L. Lampkin, "Insights and Spending Habits of Modern Grandparents," AARP, March 16, 2012, http://www.aarp.org/relationships/friends-family/info-03-2012/grandparenting-survey.html.

9. "Is A College Education Worth The Debt?" National Public Radio, September 1, 2009, http://www.npr.org/templates/story/story.php?storyId=112432364.

10. Megan McArdle, "Is College a Lousy Investment?," *Daily Beast/Newsweek*, September 9, 2012, http://www.thedailybeast.com/newsweek/2012/09/09/megan-mcardle-on-the-coming-burst-of-the-college-bubble.html.

11. Jackson Toby, "Student Loans for Dummies," *The American*, October 24, 2011, http://www.american.com/archive/2011/october/student-loans-for-dummies/article_print.

12. Devin Dwyer, "Obama: Student Loan Rate Hike Would Be 'Tremendous Blow,'" Political Punch, ABC News, April 21, 2012, http://abcnews.go.com/blogs/politics/2012/04/obama-student-loan-rate-hike-would-be-tremendous-blow/.

13. Olivier Knox, "Obama: I only paid off my student loans eight years ago," Yahoo! News, April 24, 2012, http://abcnews.go.com/Politics/OTUS/obama-paid-off-student-loans-years-ago/story?id=16204817.

14. Daniel Indiviglio, "Obama's Student-Loan Order Saves the Average Grad Less Than $10 a Month," *The Atlantic*, October 26, 2011, http://www.theatlantic.com/business/archive/2011/10/obamas-studentloan-order-saves-the-average-grad-less-than-10-a-month/247411/.

15. Emily Schultheis, "Exit polls 2012: Obama slips with youth," Politico, November 6, 2012, http://www.politico.com/news/stories/1112/83438.html.

16. "66% Oppose Forgiveness of Student Loans," Rasmussen Reports, October 25, 2011, http://www.rasmussenreports.com/public_content/politics/

general_politics/october_2011/66_oppose_forgiveness_of_student_loans.

17. Robert Costa, "Alexander: Obama's 'Soviet-Style' Takeover of Student Loans," *National Review Online*, March 30, 2010, http://www.national review.com/corner/197182/alexander-obamas-soviet-style-takeover-student-loans/robert-costa.

18. "The Quietest Trillion," *Wall Street Journal*, September 12, 2009, http://online.wsj.com/article/SB10001424052970203440104574405154157021052.html.

19. "New Low: Just 14% Think Today's Children Will Be Better Off Than Their Parents," Rasmussen Reports, July 29, 2012, http://www.rasmus senreports.com/public_content/business/jobs_employment/july_2012/new_low_just_14_think_today_s_children_will_be_better_off_than_their_parents.

20. Connie Cass, "AP-Viacom Survey of Youth on Education: American Youth See Hard Economic Times Ahead, But Remain Optimistic," *Star-Tribune*, April 18, 2011, http://www.startribune.com/nation/120079849.html?refer=y.

21. "Majority of Americans Are Upbeat About the Next Four Years," Gallup Politics, November 16, 2012, http://www.gallup.com/poll/158858/major ity-americans-upbeat-next-four-years.aspx.

22. Nicholas Eberstadt, *A Nation of Takers: America's Entitlement Epidemic* (West Conshohocken, Pennsylvania: Templeton Press, 2012), 31.

23. Phil Izzo, "Number of the Week: Half of U.S. Lives in Household Getting Benefits," *Wall Street Journal*, May 26, 2012, http://blogs.wsj.com/eco nomics/2012/05/26/number-of-the-week-half-of-u-s-lives-in-house hold-getting-benefits/.

24. Nicholas Eberstadt, "Are Entitlements Corrupting Us? Yes, American Character Is at Stake," *Wall Street Journal*, August 31, 2012, http://online.wsj.com/article/SB10000872396390444914904577619671931313542.html?mod=WSJ_hpp_RIGHTTopListofHeadlines.

25. Congressional Research Service memo, "Spending for Federal Benefits and Services for People with Low Income, FY2008-FY2011," United States Committee on the Budget (Republicans), http://budget.senate.gov/republican/public/index.cfm/files/serve/?File_id=0f87b42d-f182-4b3d-8ae2-fa8ac8a8edad.

26. Michael Barone, "Men Find Careers in Collecting Disability," RealClear-
     Politics, December 3, 2012, http://www.realclearpolitics.com/articles/
     2012/12/03/men_find_careers_in_collecting_disability_116308.html.

27. Alison Acosta Fraser, "Dependence on Government vs. the American
     Dream," Heritage Foundation, September 18, 2012, http://blog.heritage.
     org/2012/09/18/dependence-on-government-vs-the-american-dream/.

28. "About Poverty," United States Census Bureau, http://www.census.gov/
     hhes/www/poverty/about/overview/.

29. "Income, Poverty and Health Insurance in the United States: 2009–High-
     lights," United States Census Bureau, http://www.census.gov/hhes/www/
     poverty/data/incpovhlth/2009/highlights.html.

30. Hope Yen, "Millions More Americans In Poverty Than Previously Esti-
     mated: Census Bureau," Associated Press, November 14, 2012, http://
     www.huffingtonpost.com/2012/11/14/american-poverty-2012_n_
     2130544.html.

31. James Nye, "New study shows 49.7 million Americans live in poverty:
     Census Bureau release adjusted figures which reveal almost one-in-five
     struggle to survive," *Daily Mail Online*, November 14, 2012, http://www.
     dailymail.co.uk/news/article-2233137/New-study-shows-49-7-million-
     Americans-live-poverty-Census-Bureau-release-adjusted-figures-reveal-
     struggle-survive.html.

32. Editorial, "Food Stamp Nation: Uncle Sam's free grocery rolls keep grow-
     ing," *Wall Street Journal*, September 6, 2012, http://online.wsj.com/article/
     SB10000872396390443847404577631580385950886.html.

33. Senate Budget Committee chart, "Food Stamp Expenses: Doubled Since
     2008," Power Line, http://www.powerlineblog.com/admin/ed-
     assets/2011/11/FoodStampCosts.jpg.

34. Senator Jeff Sessions, "Welfare Reform Must Be Part Of Fiscal Reform,"
     United States Senate Committee on the Budget (Republicans), November
     13, 2012, http://budget.senate.gov/republican/public/index.cfm/press-
     releases?ID=8250424a-5962-4c38-b1e8-614b767aa57a.

35. Supplemental Nutrition Assistance Program chart, data as of November
     9, 2012, http://www.fns.usda.gov/pd/34SNAPmonthly.htm.

36. Tami Luhby, "Government wants more people on food stamps," CNN
     Money, June 25, 2012, http://money.cnn.com/2012/06/25/news/economy/
     food-stamps-ads/index.htm.

37. "About the Outreach Toolkits," United States Department of Agriculture, http://www.fns.usda.gov/snap/outreach/tool-kits.htm.

38. Michelle Fox, "Newt Gingrich: Obama Is 'Food Stamp President,'" CNBC, December 6, 2011, http://www.cnbc.com/id/45558774/Newt_Gingrich_ Obama_Is_Food_Stamp_President, CNBC.com.

39. "Gingrich To Chris Matthews: 'Racist' To Say Food Stamp Refers To Black," RealClearPolitics video, August 27, 2012, http://www.realclearpolitics. com/video/2012/08/27/gingrich_to_chris_matthews_racist_to_say_ food_stamp_refers_to_black.html.

40. "Pelosi: 'Food stamp president' title a 'Badge of Honor,'" Times 24/7 video, March 26, 2012, http://times247.com/24-7-videos/pelosi-food- stamp-president-title-a-badge-of-honor.

41. Teddy Davis, "Obama Shifts on Welfare Reform," Political Radar, ABC News, July 1, 2008, http://abcnews.go.com/blogs/politics/2008/07/ obama-shifts-on/.

42. Barbara Vobejda, "Clinton Signs Welfare Bill Amid Division," *Washington Post*, August 23, 1996, http://www.washingtonpost.com/wp-srv/politics/ special/welfare/stories/wf082396.htm.

43. "Clinton Signs Welfare Reform Bill, Angers Liberals," AllPolitics, CNN, http://cgi.cnn.com/ALLPOLITICS/1996/news/9608/22/welfare.sign/.

44. Editorial, "Welfare Reform as We Knew It," *Wall Street Journal*, September 29, 2012, http://online.wsj.com/article/SB100014240527023043880045 77528931414701856.html.

45. Robert Rector and Kiki Bradley, "Obama Guts Welfare Reform," Heritage Foundation, July 12, 2012, http://blog.heritage.org/2012/07/12/obama- guts-welfare-reform/.

46. "Transcript of Bill Clinton's Speech to the Democratic National Conven- tion," *New York Times*, September 5, 2012, http://www.nytimes. com/2012/09/05/us/politics/transcript-of-bill-clintons-speech-to-the- democratic-national-convention.html?pagewanted=all.

47. Olivier Knox, "White House, Obama camp, blast Romney's 'blatantly dishonest' welfare charge," Yahoo! News, August 7, 2012, http://news. yahoo.com/blogs/ticket/white-house-obama-camp-blast-romney- blatantly-dishonest-214209779.html.

48. Editorial, "Mr. Romney Hits Bottom on Welfare," *New York Times*, August 8, 2012, http://www.nytimes.com/2012/08/09/opinion/mr-romney-hits-bottom-on-welfare.html.

49. Robert Rector, "How Obama has gutted welfare reform," *Washington Post*, September 6, 2012, http://www.washingtonpost.com/opinions/how-obama-has-gutted-welfore-reform/2012/09/06/885b0092-f835-11e1-8b93-c4f4ab1c8d13_story.html.

50. Matt Cover, "GAO: Obama Administration Flip-Flopping on Welfare Waiver Authority," CNS News, September 24, 2012, http://cnsnews.com/news/article/gao-obama-administration-flip-flopping-welfare-waiver-authority.

51. Daniel Harper, "Welfare Spending Equates to $168 Per Day for Every Household in Poverty," *Weekly Standard*, December 12, 2012, http://www.weeklystandard.com/blogs/welfare-spending-equates-168-day-every-household-poverty_665160.html.

52. Veronique de Rugy, "Why Work?," *National Review Online*, December 10, 2012, http://www.nationalreview.com/corner/255012/why-work-veronique-de-rugy.

53. David Jackson, "Obama: 'I want to live in a society that's fair,'" *USA Today*, April 19, 2011, http://content.usatoday.com/communities/theoval/post/2011/04/obama-talks-debt-at-town-hall/1#.ULJ_mYc0V8E.

54. Bertrand Russell, *Sceptical Essays* (London: Routledge Classics, originally published 1928), Chapter 13.

55. David Jackson, "Obama whacks Republican economics," *USA Today*, December, 12, 2011, http://content.usatoday.com/communities/theoval/post/2011/12/obama-whacks-republican-economics/1#.ULKBCYc0V8E.

56. "If You're Willing To Work Hard You Should Be Able To Find A Good Job," RealClearPolitics video, May 10, 2012, http://www.realclearpolitics.com/video/2012/05/10/obama_if_youre_willing_to_work_hard_you_should_be_able_to_find_a_good_job.html.

57. Allegra Stratton, "David Cameron aims to make happiness the new GDP," *The Guardian*, November 14, 2010, http://www.guardian.co.uk/politics/2010/nov/14/david-cameron-wellbeing-inquiry.

58. "America's Most Miserable States," Fox Business News, March 7, 2012, http://www.foxbusiness.com/economy/2012/03/07/americas-most-miserable-states/.

59. Gary Langer, "Further Polling Data on Ryan," ABC News, August 13, 2012, http://abcnews.go.com/blogs/politics/2012/08/further-polling-data-on-ryan/.

60. Suzanne Mettler, "Our Hidden Government Benefits," *New York Times*, September 19, 2011, http://www.nytimes.com/2011/09/20/opinion/our-hidden-government-benefits.html?_r=1.

61. James Taranto, "The Social Compact," *Wall Street Journal*, April 20, 2011, http://online.wsj.com/article/SB10001424052748704658704576274993341699726.html.

62. "Biden: Girls Entitled to 'Every Single Solitary Operation,'" *Washington Free Beacon* video, October 17, 2012, http://freebeacon.com/biden-girls-entitled-to-every-single-solitary-operation/.

63. "Republicans Restricting Access to Contraception: An Estimated 20.4 Million Women Currently Benefit From Preventive Health Services Guaranteed Under The Affordable Care Act," United States Senate Democrats, http://democrats.senate.gov/republicans-restricting-access-to-contraception/.

64. Leigh Ann Caldwell, "Biden says contraception debate 'remarkable,'" *Face the Nation*, CBS News, April 1, 2012, http://www.cbsnews.com/8301-3460_162-57407577/biden-says-contraception-debate-remarkable/.

65. "Remarks by the President at a Campaign Event—Fairfax, VA," White House, October 5, 2012, http://www.whitehouse.gov/the-press-office/2012/10/05/remarks-president-campaign-event-fairfax-va.

66. "Maimonides' Eight Levels of Charity, Mishneh Torah, Laws of Charity, 10:7-14," Chabad, http://www.chabad.org/library/article_cdo/aid/45907/jewish/Eight-Levels-of-Charity.htm.

67. Erika Christakis, "Is Paul Ryan's Budget 'Un-Christian?,'" *Time*, August 14, 2012, http://ideas.time.com/2012/08/14/why-paul-ryans-budget-unchristian/.

68. Tim Mak, "Paul Ryan: Faith in the budget plan," *Politico*, April 10, 2012, http://www.politico.com/news/stories/0412/74990.html.

69. Mackenzie Weinger, "Study: Red states more charitable," *Politico*, August 20, 2012, http://www.politico.com/news/stories/0812/79888.html.

70. Robert P. George, "Law and Moral Purpose," *First Things*, January 2008, http://www.firstthings.com/article/2007/12/001-law-and-moral-purpose-16.

71. "Paul Ryan Challenged On Budget By Georgetown Faculty," *Huffington Post*, April 24, 2012, http://www.huffingtonpost.com/2012/04/24/paul-ryan-challenged-by-georgetown-faculty_n_1449437.html.

72. E. J. Dionne, "Romney's principled, radical view for America," *Washington Post*, April 25, 2012, http://www.washingtonpost.com/opinions/romneys-principled-radical-view-for-america/2012/04/25/gIQA8ZllhT_story.html.

73. Greg Sargent, "Romney-Ryan radicalism," The Plum Line, *Washington Post*, March 20, 2012, http://www.washingtonpost.com/blogs/plum-line/post/romney-ryan-radicalism/2012/03/30/gIQAy2MLlS_blog.html.

74. Joseph Knippenberg, "More on Paul Ryan and Catholic Social Teaching," First Thoughts, *First Things*, April 26, 2012, http://www.firstthings.com/blogs/firstthoughts/2012/04/26/more-on-paul-ryan-and-catholic-social-teaching/.

75. David Corn, "SECRET VIDEO: Romney Tells Millionaire Donors What He REALLY Thinks of Obama Voters," *Mother Jones*, September 17, 2012, http://www.motherjones.com/politics/2012/09/secret-video-romney-private-fundraiser.

76. Maeve Reston, "Romney reflects on his loss in call with campaign donors," *Los Angeles Times*, November 14, 2012, http://www.latimes.com/news/politics/la-pn-romney-election-campaign-donors-20121114,0,5622330.story.

77. Ginger Gibson, "Mitt Romney takes heat from GOP on 'gifts' remark," *Newsday*, November 15, 2012, http://www.newsday.com/news/nation/mitt-romney-takes-heat-from-gop-on-gifts-remark-1.4227976.

78. Katrina Trinko, "Jindal: Republicans Need to 'Go After 100 Percent of the Votes, Not 53 Percent,'" *National Review Online*, November 15, 2012, http://www.nationalreview.com/corner/333468/jindal-republicans-need-go-after-100-percent-votes-not-53-percent-katrina-trinko.

79. Paul Krugman, "Moochers Against Welfare," *New York Times*, February 16, 2012, http://www.nytimes.com/2012/02/17/opinion/krugman-moochers-against-welfare.html. (Krugman claimed that Ryan staffers were required to read the book, which is not true. We eagerly await a correction from Dr. Krugman.)

80. Jeffrey M. Stonecash, "Inequality and the American Public: Results of the Fourth Annual Maxwell School Survey Conducted September, 2007,"

Campbell Public Affairs Institute, http://www.maxwell.syr.edu/uploadedFiles/campbell/data_sources/InequalityinAmericanSociety ReportonMaxwellPollof2007.pdf.

81.   Jeanne Sahadi, "45% don't owe U.S. income tax," CNN Money, April 18, 2011, http://money.cnn.com/2011/04/14/pf/taxes/who_pays_income_taxes/index.htm.

82.   James C. Cooper, "Budget Deficit: Government Handouts Top Tax Income," *Fiscal Times*, April 18, 2011, http://www.thefiscaltimes.com/Columns/2011/04/18/Budget-Deficit-Government-Handouts-Top-Tax-Income.aspx.

83.   Myron Magnet, "The Obsolete New York Model," *City Journal*, July 2009, http://www.city-journal.org/2009/nytom_taxes.html.

84.   John Fritze, "House Dems' health bill would tax rich," *USA Today*, July 15, 2009, http://usatoday30.usatoday.com/news/health/2009-07-14-healthcare_N.htm.

85.   Stephanie Condon, "Obama: 'I Don't Want To Run Auto Companies,'" CBS News, April 29, 2009, http://www.cbsnews.com/8301-503544_162-4979228-503544.html.

86.   Becket Adams, "President Obama: Hey we 'rescued' the auto industry, why not every industry?" *The Blaze*, August 9, 2012, http://www.theblaze.com/stories/president-obama-we-rescued-the-auto-industry-why-not-every-industry/.

87.   Robert J. Samuelson, "It's the welfare state, stupid," *Washington Post*, November 11, 2012, http://www.washingtonpost.com/opinions/robert-samuelson-its-the-welfare-state-stupid/2012/11/11/e392868a-2ab0-11e2-bab2-eda299503684_story.html.

88.   Derek Thompson, "Is Our Debt Burden Really $100 Trillion?," *The Atlantic*, November 28, 2012, http://www.theatlantic.com/business/archive/2012/11/is-our-debt-burden-really-100-trillion/265644/.

Chapter 3

1.   Frank Newport, "Americans' Economic Worries: Jobs, Debt, and Politicians," Gallup Economy, January 12, 2012, http://www.gallup.com/poll/152009/americans-economic-worries-jobs-debt-politicians.aspx.

2.   Terrence P. Jeffrey, "Obama Has Now Increased Debt More than All Presidents from George Washington through George H. W. Bush Combined,"

CNS News, October 2, 2011, http://cnsnews.com/news/article/obama-has-now-increased-debt-more-all-presidents-george-washington-through-george-hw.

3.   Editorial, "Iran: How long can debt-laden US remain world power?" *Jerusalem Post*, October 18, 2012, http://www.jpost.com/IranianThreat/News/Article.aspx?id=288322.

4.   Tyrone C. Marshall Jr., "Debt is Biggest Threat to National Security, Chairman Says," American Forces Press Service, September 22, 2011, http://www.defense.gov/news/newsarticle.aspx?id=65432.

5.   "Potential Debt Problems More Common Among the Educated, Study Suggests," Ohio University, October 8, 2012, http://researchnews.osu.edu/archive/heavydebt.htm.

6.   Charles Riley, "Family net worth plummets nearly 40%," CNN Money, June 12, 2012, http://money.cnn.com/2012/06/11/news/economy/fed-family-net-worth/index.htm.

7.   Thomas Jefferson, ed. Christy Campbell, "Never Spend Your Money Before You Have It," Monticello.org, September 29, 2011, http://www.monticello.org/site/blog-and-community/posts/never-spend-your-money-before-you-have-it.

8.   Herbert Hoover, "Address to the Nebraska Republican Conference," (speech, Lincoln, Nebraska, January 16, 1936).

9.   The debt clock is available online at, http://www.usdebtclock.org/.

10.   Capital Journal, "As Budget Battle Rages On, a Quiet Cancer Grows," *Wall Street Journal*, March 8, 2011, http://online.wsj.com/article/SB10001424052748703883504576186163767307644.html.

11.   Daniel Harper, "Payments on Interest to Exceed Defense Spending by $125 Billion," *Weekly Standard*, October 23, 2012, http://www.weeklystandard.com/blogs/payments-interest-exceed-defense-spending-125-billion_657230.html.

12.   U.S. Congress, "Consolidated Appropriations Act," Library of Congress, 2012, http://www.thomas.gov/cgi-bin/query/z?c112:H.2055.enr:.

13.   Martin Crutsinger, "U.S. Deficit tops $1 Trillion for Fourth Year," Yahoo! Finance, October 12, 2012, http://finance.yahoo.com/news/us-deficit-tops-1-trillion-fourth-011445884--finance.html.

14. "The 2012 Long-Term Budget Outlook," Congressional Budget Office, June 2012, http://www.cbo.gov/sites/default/files/cbofiles/attachments/06-05-Long-Term_Budget_Outlook_2.pdf.

15. "Medicare Spending and Financing: A Primer, 2011," Kaiser Family Foundation, February 2011, www.kff.org/medicare/upload/7731-03.pdf. The GAO lists this as its more pessimistic, (or as we might view it, realistic), scenario.

16. Greg Robb, "U.S. Oct. budget deficit $120 billion: Treasury," *Wall Street Journal*, November 13, 2012, http://articles.marketwatch.com/2012-11-13/economy/35080522_1_budget-deficit-fiscal-cliff-treasury-department.

17. Anthony Rek LeCounte, "Republicans are right to resist tax-rate hike," *Daily Caller*, November 14, 2012, http://dailycaller.com/2012/11/14/republicans-are-right-to-resist-tax-rate-hikes/.

18. "Federal Gov't Now Spending $110 Billion Per Year On All Food Assistance," United States Committee on the Budgets (Republicans), http://www.budget.senate.gov/republican/public/index.cfm/charts.

19. Terence P. Jeffrey, "4 Yrs at Private College = $130,468; Median-Priced Existing Home = $173,100; U.S. Debt Per American Under 18 = $218,676," CNS News, November 4, 2012, http://cnsnews.com/news/article/4-yrs-private-college-130468-median-priced-existing-home-173100-us-debt-american-under.

20. James Pethokoukis, "Why student loans might be the next recipient of a taxpayer bailout," AEI Ideas, American Enterprise Institute, November 28, 2012, http://www.aei-ideas.org/2012/11/why-student-loans-might-be-the-next-recipient-of-a-taxpayer-bailout/.

21. Michael Tanner and Chris Edwards, "Will Obama Raise Middle-Class Taxes to Fund Health Care?" Cato Institute, June 2009, http://www.cato.org/pubs/tbb/tbb_0609-57.pdf.

22. Joshua Archambault, "Is Romneycare A Budget Buster?," Pioneer Institute, April 17th, 2012, http://www.pioneerinstitute.org/blog/news/over simplifying-the-cost-of-romneycare/.

23. Avik Roy, "CBO: Obamacare Will Spend More, Tax More, and Reduce the Deficit Less Than We Previously Thought," *Forbes*, July 7, 2012, http://www.forbes.com/sites/aroy/2012/07/27/cbo-obamacare-will-spend-more-tax-more-and-reduce-the-deficit-less-than-we-previously-thought/.

24. David Harsanyi, "Medicare and Social Security 'are on unsustainable paths,'" *Human Events*, March 27, 2012, http://www.humanevents. com/2012/04/27/medicare-social-security-on-unsustainable-paths/.

25. "2012 Annual Report of the Boards of Trustees of the Federal Hospital Insurance and Federal Supplementary Medical Insurance Trust Funds," Centers for Medicare & Medicaid Services, 2012, https://www.cms.gov/ Research-Statistics-Data-and-Systems/Statistics-Trends-and-Reports/ ReportsTrustFunds/downloads/tr2012.pdf.

26. "The 2012 OASDI Trustees Report," Social Security, December 17, 2012, http://www.ssa.gov/oact/tr/2012/index.html.

27. Ed Morrissey, "Unpatriotic Debt," *Hot Air* video, July 3, 2012, http:// hotair.com/archives/2012/07/03/video-unpatriotic-debt/.

28. Amy Payne, "Morning Bell: $16,000,000,000,000," *The Foundry*, September 5, 2012, http://blog.heritage.org/2012/09/05/morning-bell-16000000000000/.

29. Glenn Kessler, "Obama's claim that '90 percent' of the current deficit is due to Bush policies," *Washington Post*, September 26, 2012, http://www. washingtonpost.com/blogs/fact-checker/post/obamas-claim-that-90-percent-of-the-current-deficit-is-due-to-bush-policies/2012/09/26/ e9bfbcd0-077e-11e2-a10c-fa5a255a9258_blog.html.

30. Jeffrey H. Anderson, "The 7-Eleven Presidency," *Weekly Standard*, October 18, 2012, http://www.weeklystandard.com/blogs/7-eleven-presidency_654846.html.

31. David Frum, "Why I Am Not A Deficit Hawk," *Daily Beast*, April 18, 2012, http://www.thedailybeast.com/articles/2012/04/18/fiscal-hawk.html.

32. Paul Krugman, "Nobody Understands Debt," *New York Times*, January 1, 2012, http://www.nytimes.com/2012/01/02/opinion/krugman-nobody-understands-debt.html.

33. Ezra Klein, "Don't Worry About Deficit That Will Heal Itself" Bloomberg View, April 4, 2012, http://www.bloomberg.com/news/2012-04-04/dont-worry-about-deficit-that-will-heal-itself.html.

34. Joe Weisenthal, "The Untold Story Of How Clinton's Budget Destroyed The American Economy," *Business Insider*, September 5, 2012, http:// www.businessinsider.com/how-bill-clintons-balanced-budget-destroyed-the-economy-2012-9.

35. Robert Reich, "Why We Should Stop Obsessing About The Federal Budget Deficit," RobertReich.org, Novemeber 18, 2012, http://robertreich.org/post/36001609487.

36. " Obama Ag Secretary Vilsack: Food Stamps Are A 'Stimulus,'" RealClearPolitics video, August 16, 2011, http://www.realclearpolitics.com/video/2011/08/16/obama_ag_secretary_vilsack_food_stamps_are_a_stimulus.html.

37. " Carney: Unemployment Benefits Could Create Up To 1 Million Jobs," RealClearPolitics video, August 10, 2011, http://www.realclearpolitics.com/video/2011/08/10/carney_unemployment_benefits_could_create_up_to_1_million_jobs.html.

38. Ryan Dwyer "Bush tax cuts boosted federal revenue," *Washington Times*, February 3, 2010, http://www.washingtontimes.com/news/2010/feb/3/bush-tax-cuts-boosted-federal-revenue/.

39. John H. Cochrane, "CBO Demands a Leap of Faith on the Fiscal Cliff," Bloomberg View, September 3, 2012 http://www.bloomberg.com/news/2012-09-03/cbo-demands-a-leap-of-faith-on-the-fiscal-cliff.html.

40. Kim Dixon, "Buffett millionaires tax to raise $47 billion," Reuters, March 21, 2012, http://www.reuters.com/article/2012/03/21/us-usa-taxes-millionaires-idUSBRE82K0SD20120321.

41. Kerry Picket, "New book shows U.S. top earners pay larger share of taxes than any other industrialized nation," *Washington Times*, October 9, 2012, http://www.washingtontimes.com/blog/watercooler/2012/oct/9/picket-new-book-shows-us-top-earners-pay-larger-sh/#ixzz2DRQuWE6B.

42. "Statement by White House Communications Director Dan Pfeiffer on the Ryan Republican Budget," White House, March 20, 2012, http://www.whitehouse.gov/the-press-office/2012/03/20/statement-white-house-communications-director-dan-pfeiffer-ryan-republic.

43. Daniel Harper, "Obama's Plan Adds $11 Trillion to Debt," *Weekly Standard*, August 3, 2012, http://www.weeklystandard.com/blogs/obamas-plan-adds-11-trillion-debt_649279.html.

44. Alexander Bolton, "President's budget sinks, 97-0," *The Hill*, May 25, 2011, http://thehill.com/homenews/senate/163347-senate-votes-unanimously-against-obama-budget.

45.   Jeffrey M. Jones, "More in U.S. Now Want Balanced Approach to Cutting
       Deficit," Gallup Politics, November 14, 2012, http://www.gallup.com/
       poll/158828/balanced-approach-cutting-deficit.aspx.

46.   Frank James, "Obama Says He Has One Mandate: To Help The Middle
       Class," National Public Radio, November 14, 2012, http://m.npr.org/
       news/U.S./165163155.

47.   Erika Johnson, "Geithner: We should definitely just get rid of the debt
       ceiling," *Hot Air* video, November 17, 2012, http://hotair.com/
       archives/2012/11/17/geithner-we-should-definitely-just-get-rid-of-the-
       debt-ceiling/.

48.   Nick Gass, "Obama 2006 vs. Obama January 2011 vs. Obama April 2011
       on the Debt Ceiling," ABC News, April 11, 2011, http://abcnews.go.com/
       blogs/politics/2011/04/obama-2006-vs-obama-january-2011-vs-obama-
       april-2011-on-the-debt-ceiling/.

49.   Fred Backus, Sarah Dutton, Jennifer De Pinto, and Anthony Salvanto,
       "Poll: Most Americans oppose raising debt limit," CBS News, April 21,
       2011, http://www.cbsnews.com/8301-503544_162-20056258-503544.
       html.

50.   Jeanne Sahadi, "Debt ceiling FAQs: What you need to know," CNN
       Money, May 18, 2011, http://money.cnn.com/2011/01/03/news/economy/
       debt_ceiling_faqs/index.htm.

51.   Erika Johnsen, "Geithner: We should definitely just get rid of the debt
       ceiling," *Hot Air*, November 17, 2012, http://hotair.com/archives/2012/
       11/17/geithner-we-should-definitely-just-get-rid-of-the-debt-ceiling/.

52.   Kristina Wong, "President Obama: 'Every Economist from the Left and
       Right' Says Stimulus Has Saved or Created At Least Two Million Jobs,"
       Political Punch, ABC News, February 2, 2010, http://abcnews.go.com/
       blogs/politics/2010/02/president-obama-every-economist-from-the-left-
       and-right-says-stimulus-has-saved-or-created-at-least/.

53.   Mary Williams Walsh, "Illinois Debt Takes Toll, Study Finds," *New York
       Times*, October 24, 2012, http://www.nytimes.com/2012/10/25/business/
       illinois-debt-takes-toll-on-services-study-finds.html.

54.   Robert Hendin, "Coburn: U.S. 'going to get another downgrade,'" CBS
       News, May 23, 2012, http://www.cbsnews.com/8301-3460_162-
       57439931/coburn-u.s—going-to-get-another-downgrade/.

55. "Reducing Debt and Other Measures for Improving U.S. Competitiveness," National Center for Policy Analysis, November 21, 2012, http://www.ncpa.org/sub/dpd/index.php?Article_ID=22599.

56. "Geithner: Keep Politics Out of Fed's Monetary Policy," *Money News*, November 22, 2010, http://www.moneynews.com/StreetTalk/Geithner-Politics-Fed-Monetary/2010/11/22/id/377733.

Chapter 4

1. Alex Spillius, "Barack Obama criticized for 'bowing' to King Abdullah of Saudi Arabia," *The Telegraph*, April 8, 2009, http://www.telegraph.co.uk/news/worldnews/barackobama/5128171/Barack-Obama-criticised-for-bowing-to-King-Abdullah-of-Saudi-Arabia.html.

2. Associated Press, "Obama's bow in Japan sparks some criticism," MSNBC, November, 16, 2009, http://www.msnbc.msn.com/id/33978533/ns/politics-white_house/t/obamas-bow-japan-sparks-some-criticism/#. UMxvxW80V8E.

3. "Obama Draws Fire for Bow to Japanese Emperor," Fox News, November 16, 2009, http://www.foxnews.com/politics/2009/11/16/obama-draws-bow-japanese-emperor/#ixzz2F7kVyhpH.

4. Catalina Camia, "Romney jabs Obama on 'apology tour' in new ad," *USA Today*, October 23, 2012, http://www.usatoday.com/story/onpolitics/2012/10/23/romney-obama-apology-tour-ad-middle-east/1651421/.

5. "Remarks by the President to the 113th National Convention of the Veterans of Foreign Wars—Reno, Nevada," White House, July 23, 2012, http://www.whitehouse.gov/the-press-office/2012/07/23/remarks-president-113th-national-convention-veterans-foreign-wars.

6. Brent Baker, "ABC and CNN Declare 'False' What Krauthammer Touted as Romney's 'High Point,'" NewsBusters, October 23, 2012, http://newsbusters.org/blogs/brent-baker/2012/10/23/abc-and-cnn-declare-false-what-krauthammer-touted-romney-s-high-point.

7. "Text: Obama's Speech in Cairo," *New York Times*, June 4, 2009, http://www.nytimes.com/2009/06/04/us/politics/04obama.text.html.

8. "Interview with Homeland Security Secretary Janet Napolitano, 'Away From the Politics of Fear,'" *Der Spiegel*, March 16, 2009, http://www.

spiegel.de/international/world/interview-with-homeland-security-sec
retary-janet-napolitano-away-from-the-politics-of-fear-a-613330.html.

9.   Tabassum Zakaria, "General Casey: diversity shouldn't be casualty of Fort
     Hood," Reuters, November 8, 2009, http://blogs.reuters.com/tales
     fromthetrail/2009/11/08/general-casey-diversity-shouldnt-be-casualty-
     of-fort-hood/.

10. Office of the Press Secretary, "Remarks by President Obama to the Turk-
     ish Parliament," White House, April 6, 2009, http://www.whitehouse.
     gov/the_press_office/Remarks-By-President-Obama-To-The-Turkish-
     Parliament.

11. Office of the Press Secretary, "Remarks by the President at the White
     House Tribal Nations Conference," White House, December 16, 2010,
     http://www.whitehouse.gov/the-press-office/2010/12/16/remarks-
     president-white-house-tribal-nations-conference.

12. David A. Patten, "Obama: Constitution is 'Deeply Flawed,'" Newsmax,
     October 27, 2008, http://www.newsmax.com/InsideCover/obama-
     constitution/2008/10/27/id/326165#ixzz2FPn8Hg4q.

13. Jonah Goldberg, "The bashing of American exceptionalism," *Los Angeles
     Times*, November 9, 2010, http://articles.latimes.com/2010/nov/09/
     opinion/la-oe-goldberg-exceptionalism-20101109.

14. Michael Kinsley, "U.S. is not greatest country ever," Politico, November
     12, 2010, http://www.politico.com/news/stories/1110/44500.html.

15. Peter Beinart, "Election Night's Big Loser," *Daily Beast*, November 2, 2010,
     http://www.thedailybeast.com/articles/2010/11/03/how-the-gop-will-
     help-get-obama-re-elected-in-2012.html.

16. Office of the Press Secretary, "Remarks by President, Rhenus Sports
     Arena, Strasbourg, France," White House, April 3, 2009, http://www.
     whitehouse.gov/the-press-office/remarks-president-obama-strasbourg-
     town-hall.

17. "Global Opinion of Obama Slips, International Policies Faulted," Pew
     Global Attitudes Project, June 13, 2012, http://www.pewglobal.
     org/2012/06/13/chapter-2-attitudes-toward-american-culture-and-
     ideas/.

18. Peter Schwartzstein, "90 percent of Europeans would vote for Obama: poll,"
     Reuters, October 31, 2012, http://www.reuters.com/article/2012/10/31/
     us-usa-campaign-europe-idUSBRE89U19620121031.

19. Catherine Boyle and Stephane Pedrazzi, "French Socialist in Mittal Row: We're Just Doing What Obama Does," CNBC, November 30, 2012, http://www.cnbc.com/id/50022833.

20. Steve Holland and Matt Spetalnick, "Obama tells Russia's Medvedev more flexibility after election," Reuters, March 26, 2012, http://www.reuters.com/article/2012/03/26/us-nuclear-summit-obama-medvedev-idUSBRE82P0JI20120326.

21. "On World Stage, Obama Uses Podium to Express Regret," Fox News, May 12, 2009, http://www.foxnews.com/politics/2009/05/12/world-stage-obama-uses-podium-express-regret/.

22. "On World Stage, Obama Uses Podium to Express Regret," Fox News, May 12, 2009, http://www.foxnews.com/politics/2009/05/12/world-stage-obama-uses-podium-express-regret/.

23. Sangar Rahimi and Alissa J. Rubin, "Koran Burning in NATO Error Incites Afghans, *New York Times*, February 21, 2012, http://www.nytimes.com/2012/02/22/world/asia/nato-commander-apologizes-for-koran-disposal-in-afghanistan.html.

24. Alissa J. Rubin, "Obama Sends Apology as Afghan Koran Protests Rage," *New York Times*, February 23, 2012, http://www.nytimes.com/2012/02/24/world/asia/koran-burning-afghanistan-demonstrations.html.

25. Vivienne Walt, "Gaddafi vs. Switzerland: The Leader's Son on What's Behind the Feud," *Time*, February 27, 2010, http://www.time.com/time/world/article/0,8599,1968400,00.html.

26. "US apologises over Gaddafi comments," BBC News, March 9, 2010, http://news.bbc.co.uk/2/hi/africa/8558764.stm.

27. "Cairo protesters scale U.S. Embassy wall, remove flag," *USA Today*, September 9, 2012, http://content.usatoday.com/communities/ondeadline/post/2012/09/11/cairo-us-embassy-protesters-prophet-mohammad/70000126/1#.UMyBS280V8G.

28. Allahpundit, "U.S. embassy in Cairo apologizes for "abuse of free speech" after protesters tear down American flag," *Hot Air*, September 11, 2012, http://hotair.com/archives/2012/09/11/u-s-embassy-in-cairo-apologizes-for-abuse-of-free-speech-after-protesters-tear-down-american-flag/.

29. Dawn C. Chmielewski, "'Innocence of Muslims': Administration asks YouTube to review video," *Los Angeles Times*, September 13, 2012, http://

articles.latimes.com/2012/sep/13/entertainment/la-et-ct-administration-asks-youtube-to-review-innocence-of-muslims-video-20120913.

30. "Press Briefing by Press Secretary Jay Carney," White House, September 14, 2012, http://www.whitehouse.gov/the-press-office/2012/09/14/press-briefing-press-secretary-jay-carney-9142012.

31. David Jackson, "Pentagon asks pastor to pull support of anti-Islam film," *USA Today*, September 9, 2012, http://content.usatoday.com/communities/theoval/post/2012/09/12/obama-dempsey-jones/70000214/1#.UMyG3W80V8E.

32. Lucy Madison, "Hillary Clinton, Joe Lieberman Denounce Florida Pastor's Planned Quran Burning Event," CBS News, September 8, 2010, http://www.cbsnews.com/8301-503544_162-20015869-503544.html.

33. Josh Grossberg, "Innocence of Muslims Filmmaker Mark Basseley Youssef Sentenced to Death in Absentia in Egypt," E Online, November 28, 2012, http://www.eonline.com/news/366681/innocence-of-muslims-filmmaker-mark-basseley-youssef-sentenced-to-death-in-absentia-in-egypt.

34. Associated Press, "Anti-US protests continue in Pakistan, Indonesia," Fox News, September 19, 2012, http://www.foxnews.com/world/2012/09/19/anti-us-protests-continue-in-pakistan-indonesia/.

35. Staff, "Pakistan protests: US air Barack Obama advert condemning anti-Islam film," *The Telegraph*, September 21, 2012, http://www.telegraph.co.uk/news/worldnews/asia/pakistan/9557390/Pakistan-protests-US-air-Barack-Obama-advert-condemning-anti-Islam-film.html.

36. "Remarks by the President to the UN General Assembly," White House, September 25, 2012, http://www.whitehouse.gov/the-press-office/2012/09/25/remarks-president-un-general-assembly.

37. Anne Bayefsky, "You Can't Say That," *Weekly Standard*, October 5, 2009, http://weeklystandard.com/Content/Public/Articles/000/000/017/043ytrhc.asp.

38. Stephen Lee Myers, "U.S. Move to Give Egypt $450 Million in Aid Meets Resistance," *New York Times*, September 28, 2012, http://www.nytimes.com/2012/09/29/world/middleeast/white-house-move-to-give-egypt-450-million-in-aid-meets-resistance.html.

39. David D. Kirkpatrick, "Obama Walks a Fine Line With Egyptian President," *New York Times*, December 14, 2012, http://www.nytimes.com/2012/12/15/

world/middleeast/obama-walks-a-fine-line-with-egyptian-president. html.

40. Jamie Weinstein, "New York Times Cairo bureau chief: Muslim Brother-hood is 'moderate, regular old political force,'" *Daily Caller*, December 7, 2012, http://dailycaller.com/2012/12/07/new-york-times-cairo-bureau-chief-muslim-brotherhood-is-moderate-regular-old-political-force/.

41. Noah Rothman, "State Dept. Spokesperson Squirms, Eventually Contra-dicts Obama: Egypt Is An Ally," *Mediaite*, September 13, 2012, http://www. mediaite.com/columnists/state-dept-spokesperson-squirms-eventually-contradicts-obama-egypt-is-an-ally/.

42. For a detailed discussion of this see Phyllis Schlafly and George Neumayr, *No Higher Power: Obama's War on Religious Freedom* (Regnery, 2012).

43. Bruce Akerman, "Legal Acrobatics, Illegal War," *New York Times*, June 20, 2011, http://www.nytimes.com/2011/06/21/opinion/21Ackerman.html.

44. Mark Hosenball, "Exclusive: Concern grows over militant activity in Libya," Reuters, September 29, 2011, http://www.reuters.com/article/2011/09/29/ us-libya-militants-idUSTRE78S6MB20110929.

45. Borzou Daragahi, "Dialogue call to Libyan radical Islamists," *Financial Times*, September 24, 2012, http://www.ft.com/intl/cms/s/0/f02dd81e-0660-11e2-bd29-00144feabdc0.html.

46. Barak Ravid, "Barak: New U.S. intelligence report raises urgency over Iran's nuclear program," *Haaretz*, August 9, 2012, http://www.haaretz. com/news/diplomacy-defense/barak-new-u-s-intelligence-report-raises-urgency-over-iran-s-nuclear-program-1.457092.

47. Staff, "Report: Israel forced to change Iran strike tactics," *Jerusalem Post*, November 11, 2012, http://www.jpost.com/IranianThreat/News/Article. aspx?id=291295.

48. Wire, "Iran 'could make nuclear bomb within 10 months,'" *The Tele-graph*, October 12, 2012, http://www.telegraph.co.uk/news/worldnews/ middleeast/iran/9595505/Iran-could-make-nuclear-bomb-within-10-months.html.

49. Associated Press, "Iran: Nuclear enrichment advances with 'intensity,'" CBS News, November 28, 2012, http://www.cbsnews.com/8301-202_162-57555965/iran-nuclear-enrichment-advances-with-intensity/.

50. Josh Rogin, "White House opposed new Iran sanctions," *Foreign Policy*, November 30, 2012, http://thecable.foreignpolicy.com/posts/2012/11/30/white_house_opposed_new_iran_sanctions.

51. Lydia Saad, "Americans Maintain Broad Support for Israel," Gallup Politics, February 28, 2011, http://www.gallup.com/poll/146408/americans-maintain-broad-support-israel.aspx.

52. Jonathan Chait, "Why Bibi Hates Obama," *New York*, September 9, 2011, http://nymag.com/daily/intelligencer/2011/09/why_bibi_hates_obama.html.

53. Scott Wilson, "Where Obama failed on forging peace in the Middle East," *Washington Post*, July 14, 2012, http://www.washingtonpost.com/politics/obama-searches-for-middle-east-peace/2012/07/14/gJQAQQiKlW_story.html.

54. Staff, "Report: Sarkozy calls Netanyahu 'liar,'" Ynet News, November 7, 2011, http://www.ynetnews.com/articles/0,7340,L-4145266,00.html.

55. Matt Spetalnick and Allyn Fisher-Ilan, "In unusual snub, Obama to avoid meeting with Netanyahu," Reuters, September 11, 2012, http://www.reuters.com/article/2012/09/11/us-israel-iran-netanyahu-idUSBRE88A10B20120911.

56. Staff, "No time for Netanyahu—Obama's doing Letterman," YNet News, September 12, 2012, http://www.ynetnews.com/articles/0,7340,L-4280699,00.html.

57. Greta Van Susteren, "Israel: draw a clear red line!," Fox News, September 27, 2012, http://www.youtube.com/watch?feature=player_embedded&v=Ai0tcV-ShjY.

58. Jonathan S. Tobin, "Obama Blocks Out Israeli 'Noise' on Iran," *Commentary*, September 24, 2012, http://www.commentarymagazine.com/2012/09/24/obama-blocks-out-israeli-noise-on-iran/.

59. David Horovitz, "Analysis: Settlements or us," *Jerusalem Post*, March 15, 2010, http://www.jpost.com/Israel/Article.aspx?id=171007.

60. "'Meet the Press' transcript for March 14, 2010," MSNBC, http://www.msnbc.msn.com/id/35837624/ns/meet_the_press/t/meet-press-transcript-march/.

61. Mark Landler and Steven Lee Myers, "Obama Sees '67 Borders as Starting Point for Peace Deal," *New York Times*, May 19, 2011, http://www.nytimes.com/2011/05/20/world/middleeast/20speech.html.

62. "Press Briefing by Principal Deputy Press Secretary Josh Earnest," White House, July 30, 2012, http://www.whitehouse.gov/the-press-office/2012/07/30/press-briefing-principal-deputy-press-secretary-josh-earnest-7302012.

63. "Transcript: Obama's Speech at AIPAC," National Public Radio, June 4, 2008, http://www.npr.org/templates/story/story.php?storyId=91150432.

64. Glenn Kessler, "Obama Backs Away From Comment on Divided Jerusalem," *Washington Post*, June 6, 2008, http://www.washingtonpost.com/wp-dyn/content/article/2008/06/05/AR2008060503510.html.

65. Iacob Heilbrunn, "Is Mitt Romney Right About the Middle East?" *National Interest*, July 31, 2012, http://nationalinterest.org/blog/jacob-heilbrunn/mitt-romney-right-about-the-middle-east-7273.

66. Ashley Parker and Richard A. Oppel Jr., "Romney Trip Raises Sparks at a 2nd Stop," *New York Times*, July 30, 2012, http://www.nytimes.com/2012/07/31/us/politics/romney-angers-palestinians-with-comments-in-israel.html.

67. Ben Smith, "76 Senators sign on to Israel letter," *Politico*, April 13, 2010, http://www.politico.com/blogs/bensmith/0410/76_Senators_sign_on_to_Israel_letter.html.

68. Z. Byron Wolf, "Israeli Prime Minister Gets 29 Standing Ovations in Congress, Sends Message to White House," ABC News, May 24, 2011, http://abcnews.go.com/blogs/politics/2011/05/israeli-prime-minister-gets-20-standing-ovations-in-congress-sends-message-to-white-house/.

Chapter 5

1. Nancy Keenan, "Why NARAL Pro-Choice America Endorsed Barack Obama," *Huffington Post*, May 14, 2008, http://www.huffingtonpost.com/nancy-keenan/why-naral-pro-choice-amer_b_101708.html.

2. Nat Hentoff, "An abortionist's day," *Jewish World Review*, Feberuary 7, 2006, http://www.jewishworldreview.com/cols/hentoff020706.asp.

3. Colleen Raezler, "Media's Pro-Choice Darling Called Humans 'Ecotumors,'" Newsbusters, August 25, 2009, http://newsbusters.org/blogs/colleen-raezler/2009/08/25/media-s-pro-choice-darling-called-humans-ecotumors.

4. Ron Paul, *The Revolution: A Manifesto* (Grand Central Publishing, 2008), 167.

5.   "State Policies in Brief," Guttmacher Institute, March 1, 2012, http://www.
      guttmacher.org/statecenter/spibs/spib_RFU.pdf.

6.   Christopher Hitchens, *God is Not Great* (Twelve Books, 2007), 220–21.

7.   David Brody, "Obama Says He Doesn't Want His Daughters Punished
      with a Baby," The Brody File, CBN News, March 31, 2008, http://blogs.
      cbn.com/thebrodyfile/archive/2008/03/31/obama-says-he-doesnt-want-
      his-daughters-punished-with-a.aspx.

8.   "Facts on Induced Abortion in the United States," Guttmacher Institute,
      August 2011, http://www.guttmacher.org/pubs/fb_induced_abortion.
      html.

9.   Associated Press, "U.S. Abortion Rate Up Slightly After Years of Decline,"
      Fox News, January 11, 2011, http://www.foxnews.com/health/2011/01/10/
      abortion-rate-stalls-years-decline/.

10.   "Facts on Induced Abortion in the United States," Guttmacher Institute,
      August 2011, http://www.guttmacher.org/pubs/fb_induced_abortion.
      html.

11.   Lydia Saad, "More Americans 'Pro-Life' Than 'Pro-Choice' for First Time,"
      Gallup Politics, May 15, 2009, http://www.gallup.com/poll/118399/more-
      americans-pro-life-than-pro-choice-first-time.aspx.

12.   "The Complicated Politics of Abortion," Pew Research Center, August
      22, 2012, http://www.people-press.org/2012/08/22/the-complicated-
      politics-of-abortion/.

13.   "54% Are Pro-Choice, 38% Pro-Life," Rasmussen Reports, November
      14, 2012, http://www.rasmussenreports.com/public_content/politics/
      current_events/abortion/54_are_pro_choice_38_pro_life.

14.   "Obama Explains Abortion Comments," CBN News, September 8, 2008,
      http://www.cbn.com/cbnnews/politics/2008/September/Obama-
      Explains-Abortion-Comments-/.

15.   Rich Lowry, "Barack Obama the abortion extremist," Politico, August 23,
      2012, http://www.politico.com/news/stories/0812/80013.html.

16.   Barack Obama, "Obama in 2003: I'm Pro-Choice Including Late Term/
      Partial Birth Abortions," Youtube video, August 21, 2012, http://www.
      youtube.com/watch?feature=player_embedded&v=8YevBTwDqBY.

17.   Erik Eckholm, "Several States Forbid Abortion After 20 Weeks," *New York
      Times*, June 26, 2011, http://www.nytimes.com/2011/06/27/
      us/27abortion.html?_r=0.

18. Dave Andrusko, "Abortion Practitioner Gosnell to Go On Trial in March," Life News, November 4, 2012, http://www.lifenews.com/2012/11/04/ abortion-practitioner-gosnell-to-go-on-trial-in-march/.

19. David Jackson, "Obama recalls Roe v. Wade, backs abortion rights," *USA Today*, January 23, 2011, http://content.usatoday.com/communities/ theoval/post/2011/01/obama-recalls-roe-vs-wade-backs-abortion-rights/1#.UNPWxW80V8E.

20. Douglas Johnson and Susan T. Muskett, J.D., "National Right to Life White Paper: Barack Obama's Actions and Shifting Claims on the Protection of Born-Alive Aborted Infants—and What They Tell Us About His Thinking on Abortion," National Right to Life Committee, August 28, 2008, http://www.nrlc.org/ObamaBAIPA/WhitePaperAugust282008. html.

21. Ramesh Ponnuru, "Fathering More Lies," *National Review*, August 20, 2008, http://www.nationalreview.com/articles/225377/fathering-more-lies/ramesh-ponnuru.

22. "Remarks by the President at Sandy Hook Interfaith Prayer Vigil," White House, December 16, 2012, http://www.whitehouse.gov/the-press-office/2012/12/16/remarks-president-sandy-hook-interfaith-prayer-vigil.

23. Steven Ertelt, "Fluke: Ryan would let pregnant women die," *Washington Times*, September 5, 2012, http://times247.com/articles/fluke-ryan-would-let-women-die.

24. "Transcript of NARAL's Nancy Keenan remarks, Democratic National Convention," Daily Kos, September 4, 2012, http://www.dailykos.com/ story/2012/09/04/1127754/-Transcript-of-NARAL-s-Nancy-Keenan-remarks-Democratic-National-Convention.

25. "Democrats draw criticism for platform supporting abortion without exceptions," Fox News, September 04, 2012, http://www.foxnews.com/ politics/2012/09/04/democrats-draw-criticism-for-no-exceptions-abortion-platform/.

26. William Saletan, "Todd Akin's Rape Fiasco," *Slate*, August 20, 2012, http:// www.slate.com/articles/news_and_politics/frame_game/2012/08/todd_ akin_s_legitimate_rape_gaffe_shows_how_abortion_can_be_a_crime_ issue_.html.

27. Emily Deruy, "Barack Obama: 'Various Distinctions About Rape Don't Make Too Much Sense to Me'," ABC News, October 25, 2012, http://

abcnews.go.com/ABC_Univision/Politics/barack-obama-talks-
mourdock-halloween-jay-leno/story?id=17561985.

28.   Paul Stanley, "Obama on Planned Parenthood: Federal Funding Will
      Ensure 'Choice' For His Daughters," *Christian Post*, July 26, 2012, http://
      www.christianpost.com/news/obama-on-planned-parenthood-federal-
      funding-will-ensure-choice-for-his-daughters-78870/.

29.   "Annual Report 2009-2010," Planned Parenthood, http://issuu.com/
      actionfund/docs/ppfa_financials_2010_122711_web_vf?mode=windo
      w&viewMode=doublePage.

30.   Paul Bedard, "Planned Parenthood takes credit for Obama reelection,"
      Washington Examiner, November 14, 2012,: http://washingtonexaminer.
      com/planned-parenthood-takes-credit-for-obama-reelection/article/
      2513441.

31.   Bethany Monk, "Obama Administration Funds Planned Parenthood—
      Again," *Citizen Link*, July 26, 2012, http://www.citizenlink.
      com/2012/07/26/obama-administration-funds-planned-parenthood-
      again/.

32.   Carance Franke-Ruta, "A New Frontier in the Abortion Wars: Health
      Insurance," *Washington Post*, November 13, 2009, http://voices.
      washingtonpost.com/44/2009/11/a-new-frontier-opens-up-in-the.html.

33.   Phyllis Schalfly and George Neumayr have written one such a book: *No
      Higher Power: Obama's War on Religious Freedom* (Regnery, 2012).

34.   "Remarks by the President on Preventive Care," White House, February
      10, 2012, http://www.whitehouse.gov/the-press-office/2012/02/10/
      remarks-president-preventive-care.

35.   William Armstrong, Ken Smith, and Joe Aguillard. "Why We Have Gone
      to Court against the Obama Mandate," *Wall Street Journal*, April 23, 2012,
      http://www.becketfund.org/wsj-why-we-have-gone-to-court-against-
      the-obama-mandate/. Also available at http://online.wsj.com/article/SB1
      0001424052702303459004577361850557579424.html.

36.   Mary Carmichael, "New Era, New Worry," *Newsweek*, December 5, 2008,
      http://www.thedailybeast.com/newsweek/2008/12/05/new-era-new-
      worry.html.

37.   La Shawn Barber, "Marching for life and against the 'Negro Project,'"
      Townhall, January 23, 2006, http://townhall.com/columnists/lashawn-

barber/2006/01/23/marching_for_life_and_against_the_negro_project/
page/full/.

38. Michelle Charlesworth, "41% of NYC pregnancies end in abortion," ABC
     News 7, January 9, 2011, http://abclocal.go.com/wabc/
     story?section=news/local/new_york&id=7883827.

39. Steven Ertelt, "79% of Planned Parenthood Abortion Clinics Target
     Blacks, Hispanics," Life News, October 16, 2012, http://www.lifenews.
     com/2012/10/16/79-of-planned-parenthood-abortion-clinics-
     target-blacks-hispanics/.

40. "Facts on Induced Abortion in the United States," Guttmacher Institute,
     August 2011, http://www.guttmacher.org/pubs/fb_induced_abortion.
     html.

41. Steven Ertelt, "Planned Parenthood Report: $1B Group Gets 46% From
     Tax Money," Life News, December 30, 2011, http://www.lifenews.
     com/2011/12/30/planned-parenthood-report-1b-group-gets-46-from-
     tax-money/.

42. Susan Yoshihara, "Clinton Promises Global Push for Abortion Rights,"
     National Review, January 15, 2010, http://www.nationalreview.com/
     corner/192857/clinton-promises-global-push-abortion-rights/susan-
     yoshihara.

43. Amy Sullivan, "Shhh. Obama Repeals the Abortion Gag Rule, Very
     Quietly," Time, January 23, 2009, http://www.time.com/time/nation/
     article/0,8599,1873794,00.html.

Chapter 6

1.   "Remarks by the President at a Campaign Event in Roanoke, Virginia,"
     White House, July 13, 2012, http://www.whitehouse.gov/the-press-
     office/2012/07/13/remarks-president-campaign-event-roanoke-virginia.

2.   James Madison, "Federalist #51," The Federalist Papers, February 6, 1788,
     http://www.constitution.org/fed/federa51.htm.

3.   Richard Wolf, "Obama uses executive powers to get past Congress," USA
     Today, October 27, 2011, http://usatoday30.usatoday.com/news/
     washington/story/2011-10-26/obama-executive-orders/50942170/1.

INDEX